Software Engineering, Testing, and Quality Assurance for Natural Language Processing 2008

AA005263

Held in conjunction with ACL-HLT 2008

Columbus, Ohio, USA
20 June 2008

ISBN: 978-1-61738-554-4

Printed from e-media with permission by:

Curran Associates, Inc.
57 Morehouse Lane
Red Hook, NY 12571

Some format issues inherent in the e-media version may also appear in this print version.

Copyright© (2008) by the Association for Computational Linguistics
All rights reserved.

Printed by Curran Associates, Inc. (2010)

For permission requests, please contact the Association for Computational Linguistics at the address below.

Association for Computational Linguistics
209 N. Eighth Street
Stroudsburg, Pennsylvania 18360

Phone: 1-570-476-8006
Fax: 1-570-476-0860

acl@aclweb.org

Additional copies of this publication are available from:

Curran Associates, Inc.
57 Morehouse Lane
Red Hook, NY 12571 USA
Phone: 845-758-0400
Fax: 845-758-2634
Email: curran@proceedings.com
Web: www.proceedings.com

Software engineering, testing, and quality assurance for natural language processing

Software engineering in general is a first-class research object in computer science, but generally has not been treated as such within the natural language processing community. This is despite the fact that natural language as an input type has unique characteristics that present special problems for software testing, quality assurance, and even requirements specification.

The goals of this workshop included raising awareness of the need for good software engineering practices in NLP, stimulating research on same, and disseminating the results of current work in this area. We are grateful to the authors for sharing their work, and to the program committee for their efforts.

Kevin Bretonnel Cohen and Bob Carpenter

Organizers:

K. Bretonnel Cohen, The MITRE Corporation and University of Colorado School of Medicine
Bob Carpenter, Alias-i

Program Committee:

William A. Baumgartner, Jr., University of Colorado School of Medicine
Hamish Cunningham, University of Sheffield
Dan Flickinger, Stanford University
Michael Gamon, Microsoft
Martin Jansche, Google
Marc Light, Thomson
James Lyle, Microsoft
Kevin Markey, Silver Creek Systems
Stephan Oepen, Stanford University
Martha Palmer, University of Colorado at Boulder
Jeff Reynar, Google
Jun'ichi Tsujii, University of Tokyo and UK National Centre for Text Mining
Martin Volk, University of Stockholm
Scott A. Waterman, PowerSet

Additional Reviewers:

Three additional anonymous reviewers provided reviews of a submission from a workshop organizer.

Table of Contents

Workshop Program

Friday, June 20, 2008

9:00–9:10	*Welcome and opening remarks*
9:10–9:30	*Increasing Maintainability of NLP Evaluation Modules Through Declarative Implementations* Terry Heinze and Marc Light
9:30–9:50	*Type-checking in Formally Non-typed Systems* Dick Crouch and Tracy Holloway King
9:50–10:10	*zymake: A Computational Workflow System for Machine Learning and Natural Language Processing* Eric Breck
10:10–10:30	*Evaluating the Effects of Treebank Size in a Practical Application for Parsing* Kenji Sagae, Yusuke Miyao, Rune Saetre and Jun'ichi Tsujii
10:30–11:00	**Coffee break**
11:00–11:20	*Adapting Naturally Occurring Test Suites for Evaluation of Clinical Question Answering* Dina Demner-Fushman
11:20–11:40	*Software Testing and the Naturally Occurring Data Assumption in Natural Language Processing* K. Bretonnel Cohen, William A. Baumgartner Jr. and Lawrence Hunter
11:40–12:00	*Building a BioWordNet Using WordNet Data Structures and WordNet's Software Infrastructure–A Failure Story* Michael Poprat, Elena Beisswanger and Udo Hahn
12:00–2:00	**Lunch**

Friday, June 20, 2008 (continued)

2:00–2:20 *Fast, Scalable and Reliable Generation of Controlled Natural Language*
David Hardcastle and Richard Power

2:20–2:40 *Parallel Implementations of Word Alignment Tool*
Qin Gao and Stephan Vogel

2:40–3:00 *Design of the Moses Decoder for Statistical Machine Translation*
Hieu Hoang and Philipp Koehn

3:00–3:20 *Buckwalter-based Lookup Tool as Language Resource for Arabic Language Learners*
Jeffrey Micher and Clare Voss

3:30–4:00 **Coffee break**

4:00–4:20 *Reengineering a Domain-Independent Framework for Spoken Dialogue Systems*
Filipe M. Martins, Ana Mendes, Márcio Viveiros, Joana Paulo Pardal, Pedro Arez, Nuno J. Mamede and João Paulo Neto

4:20–5:00 **Open discussion session**

Increasing Maintainability of NLP Evaluation Modules Through Declarative Implementations

Terry Heinze
Research & Development Department
Thomson Corporation
Eagan, MN 55123
terry.heinze@thomson.com

Marc Light
Research & Development Department
Thomson Corporation
Eagan, MN 55123
marc.light@thomson.com

Abstract

Computing *precision* and *recall* metrics for named entity tagging and resolution involves classifying text spans as true positives, false positives, or false negatives. There are many factors that make this classification complicated for real world systems. We describe an evaluation system that attempts to control this complexity through a set of rules and a forward chaining inference engine.

1 Introduction

Computing precision and recall metrics for named entity recognition systems involves classifying each text span that the system proposes as an entity and a subset of the text spans that the gold data specifies as an entity. These text spans must be classified as true positives, false positives, or false negatives.

In the simple case, it is easy to write a procedure to walk through the list of text spans from the system and check to see if a corresponding text span exists in the gold data with the same label, mark the text span as true positive or false positive accordingly, and delete the span from the gold data set. Then the procedure need only walk through the remaining gold data set and mark these spans as false negatives. The three predicates are the equality of the span's two offsets and the labels. This evaluation procedure is useful for any natural language processing task that involves finding and labeling text spans.

The question this poster addresses is how best to manage the complexity of the evaluation system that results from adding a number of additional requirements to the classification of text spans. The requirements may include fuzzy extent predicates, label hierarchies, confidence levels for gold data, and collapsing multiple mentions in a document to produce a single classification. In addition, named entity tasks often also involve resolving a mention of an entity to an entry in an authority file (i.e., record in a relational database). This extension also requires an interleaved evaluation where the error source is important.

We started with a standard procedural approach, encoding the logic in nested conditionals. When the nesting reached a depth of five (e.g., Figure 1), we decided to try another approach. We implemented the logic in a set of rules. More specifically, we used the Drools rules and forward chaining engine (http://labs.jboss.com/drools/) to classify text spans as true positives, false positives, and/or false negatives. The procedural code was 379 lines long. The declarative system consists of 25 rules with 150 lines of supporting code. We find the rules more modular and easier to modify and maintain. However, at this time, we have no experimental result to support this opinion.

2 Added Complexity of the Classification of Text Spans for Evaluation

Matching extents and labels: A system text span may overlap a gold data span but leave out, say, punctuation. This may be deemed correct but should be recorded as a fuzzy match. A match may also exist for span labels also since they may be organized hierarchically (e.g, cities and countries are kinds of locations). Thus, calling a city a location may be considered a partial match.

Annotator Confidence: We allowed our annotators to mark text span gold data with an attribute of "low confidence." We wanted to pass this information through to the classification of the spans so that they might be filtered out for final precision and recall if desired.

Document level statistics: Some named entity tagging tasks are only interested in document level tagging. In other words, the system need only decide if an entity is mentioned in a document: how many times it is mentioned is unimportant.

Resolution: Many of our named entity tagging tasks go a step further and also require linking each entity mention to a record in a database of entities. For error anal-

Software Engineering, Testing, and Quality Assurance for Natural Language Processing, pages 1–2,
Columbus, Ohio, USA, June 2008. ©2008 Association for Computational Linguistics

ysis, we wished to note if a false negative/positive with respect to resolution is caused by the upstream named entity tagger. Finally, our authority files often have many entries for the same entity and thus the gold data contains multiple correct ids.

```
for (annotations)
  if(extents & labels match)
    if(ids match => TP res)
      if(notresolved => TN res)
      else if(single id => TP res)
      else if(multiple ids => contitional TP res)
      else error
    else
      if(gold id exists)
        if(gold id uncertain => FP res low confidence)
        else => FP res
  else
    if(fuzzy extents & labels match)
      if(ids match)
        if(no gold id => TN res)
        else if(multiple ids => conditional TP res)
        else => fuzzy TP res
      else ...
```

Figure 1: Nested conditionals for instance classification

3 Using Rules to Implement the Logic of the Classification

The rules define the necessary conditions for membership in a class. These rules are evaluated by an inference engine, which forward chains through the rule set. In this manner, rules for fuzzy matches, for handling gold data confidence factors, and for adding exclusionary conditions could be added (or removed) from the rule set without modifying procedural code.

```
rule "truepositive" salience 100
    sa : SourceAnnotation( assigned == false )
    ta : TargetAnnotation( type == sa.type,
        beginOffset == sa.beginOffset, endOffset == sa.endOffset )
  then sa.setResult("TP");
rule "false positive" salience 90
    sa : SourceAnnotation( assigned == false )
    not TargetAnnotation( type == sa.type,
        beginOffset == sa.beginOffset, endOffset == sa.endOffset )
  then sa.setResult("FP");
rule "false negative" salience 80
    ta : TargetAnnotation( assigned == false )
    not SourceAnnotation( type == ta.type,
        beginOffset == ta.beginOffset, endOffset == ta.endOffset )
  then ta.setResult("FN");
```

Figure 2: Rules for instance classification

Three rules were needed to determine the basic collection level metrics. The results of these rules were then passed on to the next sets of rules for modification for conditional checks. We use agenda groups and rule salience to control the firing precedence within the rule sets. In Figure 2, we present an example of the sort of rules that are defined.

For example, the determination of true positives was made by firing the "true positive" rule whenever an annotation from the system matched an annotation from the gold data. This occurred if the entity type and offsets were equal. This rule was given higher salience than those for true negatives and false positives since it had the effect of removing the most candidate annotations from the working memory.

Note that because we use a Java implementation that adheres to JSR94, all of the rules apply their conditions to Java objects. The syntax for tautologies within the condition statements, refer to bean properties within the enclosing object.

In Figure 3, we show first, a modification to add a fuzzy metric rule that checks false negative annotations to see if they might be a fuzzy match. Second, we show a rule that removes false positives that are defined in a stop-word list.

```
rule"fuzzy check" agenda-group "FuzzyMatch"
    ta : TargetAnnotation( result == "FN" );
    sa : SourceAnnotation( type == ta.type, result == "FP",
      ta.beginOffset < endOffset, ta.endOffset > beginOffset );
    eval(ifFuzzyMatch(sa.getText(), ta.getText(), sa.getType()));
  then sa.setResult("FzTP");
rule "filter FP" salience 10 agenda-group "Filter"
    sa : SourceAnnotation( result == "FP" );
    eval(DexterMetrics.ifStopWord(sa.getText(), sa.getType()));
  then sa.setResult(sa.getResult() + "-ignored:stop word");
```

Figure 3: Rules for modified classification

4 Conclusion

We described some of the complexities that our evaluation module had to deal with and then introduce a rule-based approach to its implementation. We feel that this approach made our evaluation code easier to understand and modify. Based on this positive experience, we suggest that other groups try using rules in their evaluation modules.

Type-checking in Formally non-typed Systems

Dick Crouch
Powerset, Inc.
San Francisco, USA
crouch@powerset.com

Tracy Holloway King
Palo Alto Research Center
Palo Alto, USA
thking@parc.com

Abstract

Type checking defines and constrains system output and intermediate representations. We report on the advantages of introducing multiple levels of type checking in deep parsing systems, even with untyped formalisms.

1 Introduction

Some formalisms have type checking as an inherent part of their theory (Copestake (2002)). However, many formalisms do not require type checking. We report on our experiences with a broad-coverage system for mapping English text into semantic representations for search applications. This system uses the XLE LFG parser for converting from text to syntactic structures and the XLE ordered-rewriting system to convert from syntax to semantic structures. Neither component formally requires type checking. However, type checking was introduced into the syntactic parser and at multiple levels in the semantics in response to the engineering requirements on a large-scale, multi-developer, multi-site system.

2 Syntactic Typing

The syntactic parser outputs a tree and an attribute value matrix (f(unctional)-structure). Meaning-sensitive applications use the f-structure which contains predicate argument relations and other semantically relevant dependencies.

A feature declaration (FD) requires every f-structure attribute to be declared with its possible values. These values are typed as to whether they are atomic or are embedded f-structures. (1) shows the FD for NUM(ber) and SPEC(ifier). NUM takes an atomic value, while SPEC takes an f-structure containing the features ADJUNCT, AQUANT, etc.

(1) a. NUM: -> $ {pl sg}.
    b. SPEC: -> << [ADJUNCT AQUANT DET NUMBER POSS QUANT SPEC-TYPE].

XLE supports overlay grammars where a grammar for an application uses another grammar as its base. The FDs form part of the overlay system. For example, there is an FD used by the Parallel Grammar project (Butt et al. (2003)); the standard English FD adds and modifies features; then domain specific FDs overlay this. (2) gives the number of features in the ParGram FD and the standard English overlay.

(2)

	atomic	f-structure
English	76	33
ParGram	34	11

The grammar cannot be loaded if there is a feature or value that is not licensed by the FD (to type check the lexicon, the generator is loaded). The command `print-unused-feature-declarations` can be used after a large parse run to determine which features never surfaced in the analysis of the corpus and hence might be candidates to be removed from the grammar.

As LFG does not have type checking as part of its theory (Dalrymple et al. (2004)), XLE originally did not implement it. However, in grammar engineering, type checking over features speeds up the development process and informs later processes and applications what features to expect since the FD serves as an overview of the output of the grammar.

Software Engineering, Testing, and Quality Assurance for Natural Language Processing, pages 3–4,
Columbus, Ohio, USA, June 2008. ©2008 Association for Computational Linguistics

3 Semantic Typing

The syntactic output is the input to several sets of ordered rewriting rules that produce semantic structures (Crouch and King (2006)). The nature of ordered rewriting systems, which consume input facts to create novel output facts, makes type checking extremely important for determining well formedness. When these representations are used in applications, type declarations can document changes so that the subsequent processing can take them into account.

The semantic typing is done by declaring every fact that can appear in the structure, its arity, and the type of its arguments. A field is available for comments and examples. (3) shows the licensing of nominal modifiers in noun-noun compounds (nn_element), where *skolem* and *integer* are argument types.

(3) |- type(proposition,
 nn_element(%%Element:skolem,
 %%Head:skolem,
 %%Nth:integer),
 comment(["%%Element is the %%Nth
 term in the compound noun %%Head
 Example {NP: the hinge oil bottle}
 in_context(t,nn_element(hinge:10,bottle:1,2))"])).

The xfr semantics is developed by multiple users. By breaking the rules into modules, type checking can occur at several stages in the processing pipeline. The current system provides for type checking at word-prime semantics, the final semantics, and abstract knowledge representation. (4) shows the number of (sub)features licensed at each level.[1]

(4)

word prime	91
lexical semantics	102
akr	45

In addition to aiding the developers of the semantics rules, the type declarations serve as documentation for the next steps in the process, e.g. creating the semantic search index and query reformulation.

4 Additional Engineering Support

The semantic type checking is a set of ordered rewrite rules, using the same mechanism as the semantics rules. As such, the notation and application are familiar to the grammar engineers and hence more accessible. Since the type checking involves additional processing time, it is not part of run-time processing. Instead, it is run within a larger regression testing regime (Chatzichrisafis et al. (2007)). Grammar engineers run a core set of regression tests before checking in any changes to the svn repository. Larger nightly runs check performance as well as typing at all levels of analysis and help ensure compatibility of changes from multiple developers.

The syntactic grammar cannot be loaded with feature type violations. However, the nature of an ordered rewriting system makes it so that loading the rules does not give the full feature type space of the resulting output. To force compliance with type checking requirements, check-ins require regression tests before committing changes. The output of these tests is type checked and, if unlicensed features are found, the commit is blocked. The grammar engineer can then update the type checking rules or modify the semantic rules to produce only licensed features. The regression testing is then rerun and, if the type checking passes, the commit proceeds.

In sum, introducing type checking at multiple levels provides a better development environment for grammar engineers as well as documentation for the developers and for applications.

[1] A stripped-down XML version of the semantics uses an xschema which checks that only the reduced feature set is used and that the XML is well-formed.

References

Butt, M., Forst, M., King, T.H. and Kuhn, J. 2003. The Feature Space in Parallel Grammar Writing. In *ESSLLI Workshop on Ideas and Strategies for Multilingual Grammar Development.*

Chatzichrisafis, N., Crouch, D., King, T.H., Nairn, R., Rayner, M. and Santaholma, M. 2007. Regression Testing for Grammar-based Systems. In *Grammar Engineering Across Frameworks.*

Copestake, A. 2002. *Implementing Typed Feature Structure Grammars.* CSLI.

Crouch, D. and King, T.H. 2006. Semantics via F-Structure Rewriting. In *Proceedings of LFG06.*

Dalrymple, M., Kaplan, R. and King, T.H. 2004. Linguistic Generalizations over Descriptions. In *Proceedings of LFG04.*

zymake: a computational workflow system for machine learning and natural language processing

Eric Breck
Department of Computer Science
Cornell University
Ithaca, NY 14853
USA
ebreck@cs.cornell.edu

Abstract

Experiments in natural language processing and machine learning typically involve running a complicated network of programs to create, process, and evaluate data. Researchers often write one or more UNIX shell scripts to "glue" together these various pieces, but such scripts are suboptimal for several reasons. Without significant additional work, a script does not handle recovering from failures, it requires keeping track of complicated filenames, and it does not support running processes in parallel. In this paper, we present zymake as a solution to all these problems. zymake scripts look like shell scripts, but have semantics similar to makefiles. Using zymake improves repeatability and scalability of running experiments, and provides a clean, simple interface for assembling components. A zymake script also serves as documentation for the complete workflow. We present a zymake script for a published set of NLP experiments, and demonstrate that it is superior to alternative solutions, including shell scripts and makefiles, while being far simpler to use than scientific grid computing systems.

1 Introduction

Running experiments in natural language processing and machine learning typically involves a complicated network of programs. One program might extract data from a raw corpus, others might preprocess it with various linguistic tools, before finally the main program being tested is run. Further programs must evaluate the output, and produce graphs and tables for inclusion in papers and presentations. All of these steps can be run by hand, but a more typical approach is to automate them using tools such as UNIX shell scripts. We argue that any approach should satisfy a number of basic criteria.

Reproducibility At some future time, the original researcher or other researchers ought to be able to re-run the set of experiments and produce identical results[1]. Such reproducibility is a cornerstone of scientific research, and ought in principle to be easier in our discipline than in a field requiring physical measurements such as physics or chemistry.

Simplicity We want to create a system that we and other researchers will find easy to use. A system which requires significant overhead before any experiment can be run can limit a researcher's ability to quickly and easily try out new ideas.

A realistic life-cycle of experiments A typical experiment evolves in structure as it goes along - the researcher may choose partway through to add new datasets, new ranges of parameters, or new sets of models to test. Moreover, a computational experiment rarely works correctly the first time. Components break for various reasons, a tool may not perform as expected, and so forth. A usable tool must be simple to use in the face of such repeated re-execution.

Software engineering Whether writing shell scripts, makefiles, or Java, one is writing code, and software engineering concerns apply. One key principle is modularity, that different parts of

[1]User input presents difficulties which we will not discuss.

Software Engineering, Testing, and Quality Assurance for Natural Language Processing, pages 5–13,
Columbus, Ohio, USA, June 2008. ©2008 Association for Computational Linguistics

training regime	classes
two-way distinction	A vs B+O
two-way distinction	B vs A+O
three-way distinction	A vs B vs O
baseline comparison	A+B vs O

Table 1: Training regimes

a program should be cleanly separated. Another is generality, creating solutions that are re-usable in different specific cases. A usable tool must encourage good software engineering.

Inherent support for the combinatorial nature of our experiments Experiments in natural language processing and machine learning typically compare different datasets, different models, different feature sets, different training regimes, and train and test on a number of cross-validation folds. This produces a very large number of files which any system must handle in a clean way.

In this paper, we present `zymake`[2], and argue that is superior to several alternatives for the task of automating the steps in running an experiment in natural language processing or machine learning.

2 A Typical NLP Experiment

As a running example, we present the following set of experiments (abstracted from (Breck et al., 2007)). The task is one of entity identification - we have a large dataset in which two different types of opinion entities are tagged, type A, and type B. We will use a sequence-based learning algorithm to model the entities, but we want to investigate the relationship between the two types. In particular, will it be preferable to learn a single model which predicts both entity type A and entity type B, or two separate models, one predicting A, and one predicting B. The former case makes a three-way distinction between entities of type A, of type B, and of type O, all other words. The latter two models make a distinction between type A and both other types or between type B and both other types. Furthermore, prior work to which we wish to compare does not distinguish at all between type A and type B, so we also need a model which just predicts entities to be of either type A or B, versus the background O. These four training regimes are summarized in Table 1.

Given one of these training regimes, the model is trained and tested using 10-fold cross-validation, and the result is evaluated using precision and recall. The evaluation is conducted separately for class A, for class B, and for predicting the union of both classes.

2.1 Approach 1: A UNIX Shell Script

Many researchers use UNIX shell scripts to co-ordinate experiments[3]. Figure 1 presents a potential shell script for the experiments discussed in Section 2. Shell scripting is familiar and widely used for co-ordinating the execution of programs. However, there are three difficulties with this approach - it is difficult to partially re-run, the specification of the filenames is error-prone, and the script is badly modularized.

Re-running the experiment The largest difficulty with this script is how it handles errors - namely, it does not. If some early processes succeed, but later ones fail, the researcher can only re-run the entire script, wasting the time spent on the previous run. There are two common solutions to this problem. The simplest is to comment out the parts of the script which have succeeded, and re-run the script. This is highly brittle and error-prone. More reliable but much more complicated is to write a wrapper around each command which checks whether the outputs from the command already exist before running it. Neither of these is desirable. It is also worth noting that this problem can arise not just through error, but when an input file changes, an experiment is extended with further processing, additional graphs are added, further statistics are calculated, or if another model is added to the comparison.

[2]Any name consisting of a single letter followed by `make` already refers to an existing software project. `zymake` is the first pronouncable name consisting of a two letter prefix to `make`, starting from the end of the alphabet. I pronounce "zy-" as in "zydeco."

[3]Some researchers use more general programming languages, such as Perl, Python, or Java to co-ordinate their experiments. While such languages may make some aspects of co-ordination easier – for example, such languages would not have to call out to an external program to produce a range of integers as does the script in Figure 1 – the arguments that follow apply equally to these other approaches.

```
for fold in `seq 0 9`; do
  extract-test-data $fold raw-data $fold.test
  for class in A B A+B; do
    extract-2way-training $fold raw-data $class > $fold.$class.train
    train $fold.$class.train > $fold.$class.model
    predict $fold.$class.model $fold.test > $fold.$class.out
    prep-eval-2way $fold.$class.out > $fold.eval-in
    eval $class $fold.$class.eval-in > $fold.$class.eval
  done
  extract-3way-training $fold raw-data > $fold.3way.train
  train $fold.3way.train > $fold.3way.model
  predict $fold.3way.model $fold.test > $fold.3way.out
  for class in A B A+B; do
    prep-eval-3way $class $fold.3way.out > $fold.3way.$class.eval-in
    eval $class $fold.3way.$class.eval-in > $fold.3way.$class.eval
  done
done
```

Figure 1: A shell script

Problematic filenames In this example, a filename is a concatenation of several variable names - e.g. `$(fold).$(class).train`. This is also error-prone - the writer of the script has to keep track, for each filename, of which attributes need to be specified for a given file, and the order in which they must be specified. Either of these can change as an experiment's design evolves, and subtle design changes can require changes throughout the script of the references to many filenames.

Bad modularization In this example, the `eval` program is called twice, even though the input and output files in each case are of the same format. The problem is that the filenames are such that the line in the script which calls `eval` needs to be include information about precisely which files (in one case `$fold.3way.$class`, and in the other `$fold.$class`) are being evaluated. This is irrelevant – a more modular specification for the `eval` program would simply say that it operates on a `.eval-in` file and produces an `.eval` file. We will see ways below of achieving exactly this.[4]

[4]One way of achieving this modularization with shell scripts could involve defining functions. While this could be effective, this greatly increases the complexity of the scripts.

```
%.model: %.train
  train $< > $@

%.out: %.model %.test
  predict $^ > $@
```

Figure 2: A partial makefile

2.2 Approach 2: A `makefile`

One solution to the problems detailed above is to use a makefile instead of a shell script. The `make` program (Feldman, 1979) bills itself as a "utility to maintain groups of programs"[5], but from our perspective, `make` is a declarative language for specifying dependencies. This seems to be exactly what we want, and indeed it does solve some of the problems detailed above. `make` has several new problems, though, which result in its being not an ideal solution to our problem.

Figure 2 presents a portion of a makefile for this task. For this part, the makefile ideally matches what we want. It will pick up where it left off, avoiding the re-running problem above. The question of filenames is sidestepped, as we only need to deal with the extensions here. And each command is neatly

[5]GNU `make` manpage.

partitioned into its own section, which specifies its dependencies, the files created by each command, and the shell command to run to create them. However, there are three serious problems with this approach.

Files are represented by strings The first problem can be seen by trying to write a similar line for the `eval` command. It would look something like this:

```
%.eval: %.eval-in
  eval get-class $^ > $@
```

However, it is hard to write the code represented here as `get-class`. This code needs to examine the filename string of `$^` or `$@`, and extract the class from that. This is certainly possible using standard UNIX shell tools or make extensions, but it is ugly, and has to be written once for every time such a field needs to be accessed. For example, one way of writing `get-class` using GNU make extensions would be:

```
GETCLASS = $(filter A B A+B,\
$(subst ., ,$(1)))

%.eval: %.eval-in
  eval $(call GETCLASS,$@) $^ > $@
```

The basic problem here is that to `make`, a file is represented by a string, its filename. For machine learning and natural language processing experiments, it is much more natural to represent a file as a set of key-value pairs. For example, the file `0.B.model` might be represented as { `fold = 0, class = B, filetype = model` } .

Combinatorial dependencies The second problem with `make` is that it is very difficult to specify combinatorial dependencies. If one continued to write the makefile above, one would eventually need to write a final `all` target to specify all the files which would need to be built. There are 60 such files: one for each fold of the following set

```
$fold.3way.A.eval
$fold.3way.B.eval
$fold.3way.A+B.eval
$fold.A.eval
$fold.B.eval
$fold.A+B.eval
```

There is no easy way in `make` of listing these 60 files in a natural manner. One can escape to a shell script, or use GNU `make`'s `foreach` function, but both ways are messy.

Non-representable dependency structures The final problem with `make` also relates to dependencies. It is more subtle, but it turns out that there are some sorts of dependency structures which cannot be represented in `make`. Suppose I want to compare the effect of using one of three parsers, one of three part-of-speech-taggers and one of three chunkers for a summarization experiment. This involves three separate three-way distinctions in the makefile, where for each, there are three different commands that might be run. A non-working example is in Fig-

```
%.taggerA.pos: %.txt
  tagger_A $^ > $@

%.taggerB.pos: %.txt
  tagger_B $^ > $@

%.taggerC.pos: %.txt
  tagger_C $^ > $@

%.chunkerA.chk: %.pos
  chunker_A $^ > $@

%.chunkerB.chk: %.pos
  chunker_B $^ > $@

%.chunkerC.chk: %.pos
  chunker_C $^ > $@

%.parserA.prs: %.chk
  parser_A $^ > $@

%.parserB.prs: %.chk
  parser_B $^ > $@

%.parserC.prs: %.chk
  parser_C $^ > $@
```

Figure 3: A non-functional makefile for testing three independent decisions

ure 3. The problem is that `make` pattern rules (rules using the `%` character) can only match the suffix or prefix of a filename[6]. This makefile does not work because it requires the parser, chunker, and tagger to all be the last part of the filename before the type suffix.

2.3 Approach 3: `zymake`

`zymake` is designed to address the problems outlined above. The key principles of its design are as follows:

- Like `make`, `zymake`files can be re-run multiple times, each time picking up where the last left off.
- Files are specified by key-value sets, not by strings
- `zymake` includes a straightforward way of handling combinatorial sets of files.
- `zymake` syntax is minimally different from shell syntax.

Figure 4 presents a zymakefile which runs the running example experiment. Rather than explaining the entire file at once, we will present a series of increasingly complex parts of it.

Figure 5 presents the simplest possible zymakefile, consisting of one *rule*, which describes how to create a `$().test` file, and one *goal*, which lists what files should be created by this file. A rule is simply a shell command[7], with some number of *interpolations*[8]. An *interpolation* is anything between the characters `$(` and the matching `)`. This is the only form of interpolation done by `zymake`, so as to minimally conflict with other interpolations done by the shell, scripting languages such as Perl, etc.

[6]Thus, if we were only comparing two sets of items – e.g. parsers and taggers but not chunkers – we could write this set of dependencies by using a prefix to distinguish one set and a suffix to distinguish the other. This is hardly pretty, though, and does not extend to more than two sets.

[7]Users who are familiar with UNIX shells will find it useful to be able to use input/output redirection and pipelines in zymakefiles. Knowledge of advanced shell programming is not necessary to use `zymake`, however.

[8]This term is used in Perl; it is sometimes referred to in other languages as "substitution" or "expansion."

```
extract-test-data $(fold) raw-data
 $(>).test

extract-2way-training $(fold) raw-data
 $(class) > $(train="2way").train

extract-3way-training $(fold) raw-data
  > $(train="3way").train

train $().train > $().model

predict $().model $().test > $().out

prep-eval-3way $(class) $().out >
  $(train="3way").eval-in

prep-eval-2way $().out >
  $(train="2way").eval-in

eval $(class) $().eval-in > $().eval

classes = A B A+B
ways = 2way 3way

: $(fold = *(range 0 9)
    class = *classes
    train = *ways).eval
```

Figure 4: An example zymakefile. The exact commands run by this makefile are presented in Appendix A.

```
extract-test-data raw-data $(>).test

: $().test
```

Figure 5: Simple zymakefile #1

```
extract-test-data $(fold) raw-data
 $(>).test

: $(fold=0).test $(fold=1).test
```

Figure 6: Simple zymakefile #2

```
extract-test-data $(fold) raw-data
$(>).test

folds = 0 1

: $(fold=*folds).test
```

Figure 7: Simple zymakefile #3

The two interpolations in this example are file interpolations, which are replaced by `zymake` with a generated filename. Files in `zymake` are identified not by a filename string but by a set of key-value pairs, along with a suffix. In this case, the two interpolations have no key-value pairs, and so are only represented by a suffix. Finally, there are two kinds of file interpolations - *inputs*, which are files that are required to exist before a command can be run, and *outputs*, which are files created by a command[9]. In this case, the interpolation `$(>).test` is marked as an output by the > character[10], while `$().test` is an input, since it is unmarked.

The goal of this program is to create a file matching the interpolation `$().test`. The single rule does create a file matching that interpolation, and so this program will result in the execution of the following single command:

```
extract-test-data raw-data .test
```

Figure 6 presents a slightly more complex zymakefile. In this case, there are two goals - to create a `.test` file with the key `fold` having the value `0`, and another `.test` file with `fold` equal to `1`. We also see that the rule has become slightly more complex – there is now another interpolation. This, however, is not a file interpolation, but a variable interpolation. `$(fold)` will be replaced by the value of `fold`.

[9]Unlike `make`, `zymake` requires that each command explicitly mention an interpolation corresponding to each input or output file. This restriction is caused by the merging of the command part of the rule with the dependency part of the rule, which are separate in `make`. We felt that this reduced redundancy and clutter in the zymakefiles, but this may occasionally require writing a wrapper around a program which does not behave in this manner.

[10]`zymake` will also infer that any file interpolation following the > character, representing standard output redirection in the shell, is an output

Executing this zymakefile results in the execution of two commands:

```
extract-test-data 0 raw-data 0.test
extract-test-data 1 raw-data 1.test
```

Note that the output files are now not just `.test` but include the fold number in their name. This is because `zymake` infers that the fold key, mentioned in the extract rule, is needed to distinguish the two test files. In general the user should specify as few keys as possible for each file interpolation, and allow `zymake` to infer the exact set of keys necessary to distinguish each file from the rest[11].

Figure 7 presents a small refinement to the zymakefile in Figure 6. The commands that will be run are the same, but instead of separately listing the two test files to be created, we create a variable `folds` which is a list of all the folds we want, and use a *splat* to create multiple goals. A splat is indicated by the asterisk character, and creates one copy of the file interpolation for each value in the variable's list.

Figure 4 is now a straightforward extension of the example we have seen so far. It uses a few more features of `zymake` that we will not discuss, such as string-valued keys, and the `range` function, but further documentation is available on the `zymake` website. `zymake` wants to create the goals at the end, so it examines all the rules and constructs a *directed acyclic graph*, or *DAG*, representing the dependencies among the files. It then executes the commands in some order based on this DAG – see Section 3 for discussion of execution order.

2.4 Benefits of `zymake`

`zymake` satisfies the criteria set out above, and handles the problems discussed with other systems.

- *Reproducibility.* By providing a single file which can be re-executed many times, `zymake` encourages a development style that encodes all information about a workflow in a single file. This also serves as documentation of the complete workflow.

[11]Each file will be distinguished by all and only the keys needed for the execution of the command that created it, and the commands that created its inputs. A unique, global ordering of keys is used along with a unique, global mapping of filename components to key, value pairs so that the generated filename for each file uniquely maps to the appropriate set of key, value pairs.

- *Simplicity.* zymake only requires writing a set of shell commands, annotated with interpolations. This allows researchers to quickly and easily construct new and more complex experiments, or to modify existing ones.
- *Experimental life-cycle.* zymake can re-execute the same file many times when components fail, inputs change, or the workflow is extended.
- *Software engineering.* Each command in a zymakefile only needs to describe the inputs and outputs relevant for that command, making the separate parts of the file quite modular.
- *Combinatorial experiments.* zymake includes a built-in method for specifying that a particular variable needs to range over several possibilities, such as a set of models, parameter values, or datasets.

2.5 Using zymake

Beginning to use zymake is as simple as downloading a single binary from the website[12]. Just as with a shell script or makefile, the user then writes a single textual zymakefile, and passes it to zymake for execution. Typical usage of zymake will be in an edit-run development cycle.

3 Parallel Execution

For execution of very large experiments, efficient use of parallelism is necessary. zymake offers a natural way of executing the experiment in a maximally parallel manner. The default serial execution does a topological sort of the DAG, and executes the components in that order. To execute in parallel, zymake steps through the DAG starting at the roots, starting any command which does not depend on a command which has not yet executed.

To make this practical, of course, remote execution must be combined with parallel execution. The current implementation provides a simple means of executing a remote job using ssh, combined with a simple /proc-based measure of remote cpu utilization to find the least-used remote cpu from a provided set. We are currently looking at extending zymake to interface it with the Condor system (Litzkow et al., 1988). Condor's DAGMan is designed to execute a DAG in parallel on a set of remote machines, so it should naturally fit with zymake. Interfaces to other cluster software are possible as well. Another important extension will be to allow the system to throttle the number of concurrent jobs produced and/or collect smaller jobs together, to better match the available computational resources.

4 Other approaches

Deelman et al. (2004) and Gil et al. (2007) describe the Pegasus and Wings systems, which together have a quite similar goal to zymake. This system is designed to manage large scientific workflows, with both data and computation distributed across many machines. A user describes their available data and resources in a semantic language, along with an abstract specification of a workflow, which Wings then renders into a complete workflow DAG. This is passed to Pegasus, which instantiates the DAG with instances of the described resources and passes it to Condor for actual execution. The system has been used for large-scale scientific experiments, such as earthquake simulation. However, we believe that the added complexity of the input that a user has to provide over zymake's simple shell-like syntax will mean a typical machine learning or natural language processing researcher will find zymake easier to use.

The GATE and UIMA architectures focus specifically on the management of components for language processing (Cunningham et al., 2002; Ferrucci and Lally, 2004). While zymake knows nothing about the structure of the files it manages, these systems provide a common format for textual annotations which all components must use. GATE provides a graphical user interface for running components and for viewing and producing annotations. UIMA provides a framework not just for running experiments but for data analysis and application deployment. Compared to writing a zymake script, however, the requirements for using these systems to manage an experiment are greater. In addition, both these architectures most naturally support com-

[12]Binaries for Linux, Mac OS X, and Windows, as well as full source code, are available at http://www.cs.cornell.edu/~ebreck/zymake/.

ponents written in Java (and in the case of UIMA, C++). zymake is agnostic as to the source language of each component, making it easier to include programs written by third parties or by researchers who prefer different languages.

make, despite dating from 1979, has proved its usefulness over time, and is still widely used. Many other systems have been developed to replace it, including ant[13], SCons[14], maven[15], and others. However, so far as we are aware, none of these systems solves the problems we have described with make. As with make and shell scripts, running experiments is certainly possible using these other tools, but we believe they are far more complex and cumbersome than zymake.

5 Future Extensions

There are a number of extensions to zymake which could make it even more useful. One is to allow the dependency DAG to vary during the running of the experiment. At the moment, zymake requires that the entire DAG be known before any processes can run. As an example of when this is less than ideal, consider early-stopping an artificial neural network. One way of doing this is train the network to full convergence, and output predictions from the intermediate networks at some fixed interval of epochs. We would like then to evaluate all these predictions on held-out data (running one process for each of them) and then to choose the point at which this score is maximized (running one process for the whole set). Since the number of iterations to convergence is not known ahead of time, at the moment we cannot support this structure in zymake. We plan, however, to allow the structure of the DAG to vary at run-time, allowing such experiments.

We are also interested in other extensions, including an optional textual or graphical progress bar, providing a way for the user to have more control over the string filename produced from a key-value set[16], and keeping track of previous versions of created files, to provide a sort of version control of the output files.

[13] http://ant.apache.org/.

[14] http://www.scons.org/.

[15] http://maven.apache.org/.

[16] This will better allow zymake to interact with other workflows.

6 Conclusion

Most experiments in machine learning and natural language processing involve running a complex, interdependent set of processes. We have argued that there are serious difficulties with common approaches to automating these experiments. In their place, we offer zymake, a new scripting language with shell-like syntax but make-like semantics. We hope our community will find it as useful as we have.

Acknowledgements

We thank Yejin Choi, Alex Niculescu-Mizil, David Pierce, the Cornell machine learning discussion group, and the anonymous reviewers for helpful comments on earlier drafts of this paper.

A Output of Figure 4

We present here the commands run by zymake when presented with the file in Figure 4. We present only the commands run for fold 0, not for all 10 folds. Also, in actual execution zymake adds a prefix to each filename based on the name of the zymakefile, so as to separate different experiments. Finally, note that this is only one possible order that the commands could be run in.

```
extract-2way-training 0 raw-data A > A.0.2way.train
train A.0.2way.train > A.0.2way.model
extract-2way-training 0 raw-data B > B.0.2way.train
train B.0.2way.train > B.0.2way.model
extract-2way-training 0 raw-data A+B > AB.0.2way.tra
train AB.0.2way.train > AB.0.2way.model
extract-3way-training 0 raw-data > 0.3way.train
train 0.3way.train > 0.3way.model
extract-test-data 0 raw-data 0.test
predict A.0.2way.model 0.test > A.0.2way.out
prep-eval-2way A.0.2way.out > A.0.2way.eval-in
eval A A.0.2way.eval-in > A.0.2way.eval
predict B.0.2way.model 0.test > B.0.2way.out
prep-eval-2way B.0.2way.out > B.0.2way.eval-in
eval B B.0.2way.eval-in > B.0.2way.eval
predict AB.0.2way.model 0.test > AB.0.2way.out
prep-eval-2way AB.0.2way.out > AB.0.2way.eval-in
eval A+B AB.0.2way.eval-in > AB.0.2way.eval
predict 0.3way.model 0.test > 0.3way.out
prep-eval-3way A 0.3way.out > A.0.3way.eval-in
eval A A.0.3way.eval-in > A.0.3way.eval
prep-eval-3way B 0.3way.out > B.0.3way.eval-in
eval B B.0.3way.eval-in > B.0.3way.eval
prep-eval-3way A+B 0.3way.out > AB.0.3way.eval-in
eval A+B AB.0.3way.eval-in > AB.0.3way.eval
```

References

Eric Breck, Yejin Choi, and Claire Cardie. 2007. Identifying expressions of opinion in context. In *Proceedings of the Twentieth International Joint Conference on Artificial Intelligence (IJCAI-2007)*, Hyderabad, India, January.

Hamish Cunningham, Diana Maynard, Kalina Bontcheva, and Valentin Tablan. 2002. GATE: A framework and graphical development environment for robust NLP tools and applications. In *Proceedings of the 40th Anniversary Meeting of the Association for Computational Linguistics (ACL '02)*, Philadelphia, July.

Ewa Deelman, James Blythe, Yolanda Gil, Carl Kesselman, Gaurang Mehta, Sonal Patil, Mei-Hui Su, Karan Vahi, and Miron Livny. 2004. Pegasus : Mapping scientific workflows onto the grid. In *Across Grids Conference*, Nicosia, Cyprus.

Stuart I. Feldman. 1979. Make-a program for maintaining computer programs. *Software - Practice and Experience*, 9(4):255–65.

David Ferrucci and Adam Lally. 2004. UIMA: an architectural approach to unstructured information processing in the corporate research environment. *Nat. Lang. Eng.*, 10(3-4):327–348.

Yolanda Gil, Varun Ratnakar, Ewa Deelman, Gaurang Mehta, and Jihie Kim. 2007. Wings for pegasus: Creating large-scale scientific applications using semantic representations of computational workflows. In *Proceedings of the 19th Annual Conference on Innovative Applications of Artificial Intelligence (IAAI)*, Vancouver, British Columbia, Canada, July.

Michael Litzkow, Miron Livny, and Matthew Mutka. 1988. Condor - a hunter of idle workstations. In *Proceedings of the 8th International Conference of Distributed Computing Systems*, June.

Evaluating the Effects of Treebank Size in a Practical Application for Parsing

Kenji Sagae[1], **Yusuke Miyao**[1], **Rune Sætre**[1] and **Jun'ichi Tsujii**[1,2,3]
[1]Department of Computer Science, Univerisity of Tokyo, Japan
[2]School of Computer Science, University of Manchester
[3]National Center for Text Mining, Manchester, UK
{sagae,yusuke,rune.saetre,tsujii@is.s.u-tokyo.ac.jp}

Abstract

Natural language processing modules such as part-of-speech taggers, named-entity recognizers and syntactic parsers are commonly evaluated in isolation, under the assumption that artificial evaluation metrics for individual parts are predictive of practical performance of more complex language technology systems that perform practical tasks. Although this is an important issue in the design and engineering of systems that use natural language input, it is often unclear how the accuracy of an end-user application is affected by parameters that affect individual NLP modules. We explore this issue in the context of a specific task by examining the relationship between the accuracy of a syntactic parser and the overall performance of an information extraction system for biomedical text that includes the parser as one of its components. We present an empirical investigation of the relationship between factors that affect the accuracy of syntactic analysis, and how the difference in parse accuracy affects the overall system.

1 Introduction

Software systems that perform practical tasks with natural language input often include, in addition to task-specific components, a pipeline of basic natural language processing modules, such as part-of-speech taggers, named-entity recognizers, syntactic parsers and semantic-role labelers. Although such building blocks of larger language technology solutions are usually carefully evaluated in isolation using standard test sets, the impact of improvements in each individual module on the overall performance of end-to-end systems is less well understood. While the effects of the amount of training data, search beam widths and various machine learning frameworks have been explored in detail with respect to speed and accuracy in basic natural language processing tasks, how these trade-offs in individual modules affect the performance of the larger systems they compose is an issue that has received relatively little attention. This issue, however, is of great practical importance in the effective design and engineering of complex software systems that deal with natural language.

In this paper we explore some of these issues empirically in an information extraction task in the biomedical domain, the identification of protein-protein interactions (PPI) mentioned in papers abstracts from MEDLINE, a large database of biomedical papers. Due in large part to the creation of biomedical treebanks (Kulick et al., 2004; Tateisi et al., 2005) and rapid progress of data-driven parsers (Lease and Charniak, 2005; Nivre et al., 2007), there are now fast, robust and accurate syntactic parsers for text in the biomedical domain. Recent research shows that parsing accuracy of biomedical corpora is now between 80% and 90% (Clegg and Shepherd, 2007; Pyysalo et al., 2007; Sagae et al., 2008). Intuitively, syntactic relationships between words should be valuable in determining possible interactions between entities present in text. Recent PPI extraction systems have confirmed this intuition (Erkan et al., 2007; Sætre et al., 2007; Katrenko and Adriaans, 2006).

While it is now relatively clear that syntactic parsing is useful in practical tasks that use natural language corpora in bioinformatics, several ques-

Software Engineering, Testing, and Quality Assurance for Natural Language Processing, pages 14–20,
Columbus, Ohio, USA, June 2008. ©2008 Association for Computational Linguistics

tions remain as to research issues that affect the design and testing of end-user applications, including how syntactic analyses should be used in a practical setting, whether further improvements in parsing technologies will result in further improvements in practical systems, whether it is important to continue the development of treebanks and parser adaptation techniques for the biomedical domain, and how much effort should be spent on comparing and benchmarking parsers for biomedical data. We attempt to shed some light on these matters by presenting experiments that show the relationship of the accuracy of a dependency parser and the accuracy of the larger PPI system that includes the parser. We investigate the effects of domain-specific treebank size (the amount of available manually annotated training data for syntactic parsers) and final system performance, and obtain results that should be informative to researchers in bioinformatics who rely on existing NLP resources to design information extraction systems, as well as to members of the parsing community who are interested in the practical impact of parsing research.

In section 2 we discuss our motivation and related efforts. Section 3 describes the system for identification of protein-protein interactions used in our experiments, and in section 4 describes the syntactic parser that provides the analyses for the PPI system, and the data used to train the parser. We describe our experiments, results and analysis in section 5, and conclude in section 6.

2 Motivation and related work

While recent work has addressed questions relating to the use of different parsers or different types of syntactic representations in the PPI extraction task (Sætre et al., 2007, Miyao et al., 2008), little concrete evidence has been provided for potential benefits of improved parsers or additional resources for training syntactic parsers. In fact, although there is increasing interest in parser evaluation in the biomedical domain in terms of precision/recall of brackets and dependency accuracy (Clegg and Shepherd, 2007; Pyysalo et al., 2007; Sagae et al., 2008), the relationship between these evaluation metrics and the performance of practical information extraction systems remains unclear. In the parsing community, relatively small accuracy gains are often reported as success stories, but again, the precise impact of such improvements on practical tasks in bioinformatics has not been established.

One aspect of this issue is the question of domain portability and domain adaptation for parsers and other NLP modules. Clegg and Shepherd (2007) mention that available statistical parsers appear to overfit to the newswire domain, because of their extensive use of the Wall Street Journal portion of the Penn Treebank (Marcus et al., 1994) during development and training. While this claim is supported by convincing evaluations that show that parsers trained on the WSJ Penn Treebank alone perform poorly on biomedical text in terms of accuracy of dependencies or bracketing of phrase structure, the benefits of using domain-specific data in terms of practical system performance have not been quantified. These expected benefits drive the development of domain-specific resources, such as the GENIA treebank (Tateisi et al., 2005), and parser domain adaption (Hara et al., 2007), which are of clear importance in parsing research, but of largely unconfirmed impact on practical systems.

Quirk and Corston-Oliver (2006) examine a similar issue, the relationship between parser accuracy and overall system accuracy in syntax-informed machine translation. Their research is similar to the work presented here, but they focused on the use of varying amounts of out-of-domain training data for the parser, measuring how a translation system for technical text performed when its syntactic parser was trained with varying amounts of Wall Street Journal text. Our work, in contrast, investigates the use of domain-specific training material in parsers for biomedical text, a domain where significant amounts of effort are allocated for development of domain-specific NLP resources in hope that such resources will result in better overall performance in practical systems.

3 A PPI extraction system based on syntactic parsing

PPI extraction is an NLP task to identify protein pairs that are mentioned as interacting in biomedical papers. Figure 2 shows two sentences that include protein names: the former sentence mentions a protein interaction, while the latter does not. Given a protein pair, PPI extraction is a task of binary classification; for example, <IL-8, CXCR1>

> This study demonstrates that **IL-8** recognizes and activates **CXCR1**, **CXCR2**, and the **Duffy antigen** by distinct mechanisms.
>
> The molar ratio of serum **retinol-binding protein** (**RBP**) to **transthyretin** (**TTR**) is not useful to assess vitamin A status during infection in hospitalized children.

Figure 2: Example sentences with protein names

is a positive example, and <RBP, TTR> is a negative example.

Following recent work on using dependency parsing in systems that identify protein interactions in biomedical text (Erkan et al., 2007; Sætre et al., 2007; Katrenko and Adriaans, 2006), we have built a system for PPI extraction that uses dependency relations as features. As exemplified, for the protein pair **IL-8** and **CXCR1** in the first sentence of Figure 2, a dependency parser outputs a dependency tree shown in Figure 1. From this dependency tree, we can extract a dependency path between **IL-8** and **CXCR1** (Figure 3), which appears to be a strong clue in knowing that these proteins are mentioned as interacting.

The system we use in this paper is similar to the one described in Sætre et al. (2007), except that it uses syntactic dependency paths obtained with a dependency parser, but not predicate-argument paths based on deep-parsing. This method is based on SVM with SubSet Tree Kernels (Collins, 2002; Moschitti, 2006). A dependency path is encoded as a flat tree as depicted in Figure 4. Because a tree kernel measures the similarity of trees by counting common subtrees, it is expected that the system finds effective subsequences of dependency paths. In addition to syntactic dependency features, we incorporate bag-of-words features, which are regarded as a strong baseline for IE systems. We use lemmas of words before, between and after the pair of target proteins.

In this paper, we use Aimed (Bunescu and Mooney, 2004), which is a popular benchmark for the evaluation of PPI extraction systems. The Aimed corpus consists of 225 biomedical paper abstracts (1970 sentences), which are sentence-

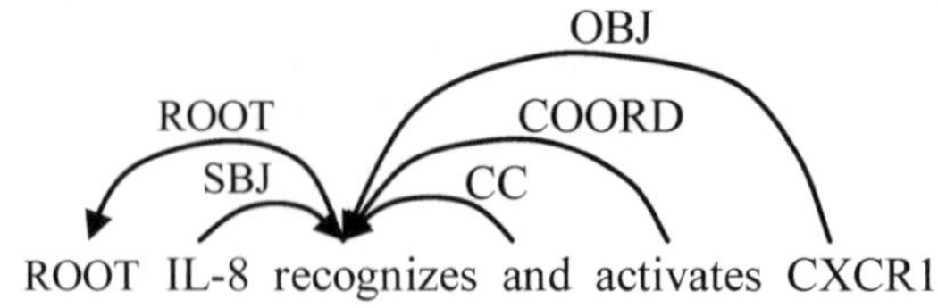

Figure 1: A dependency tree

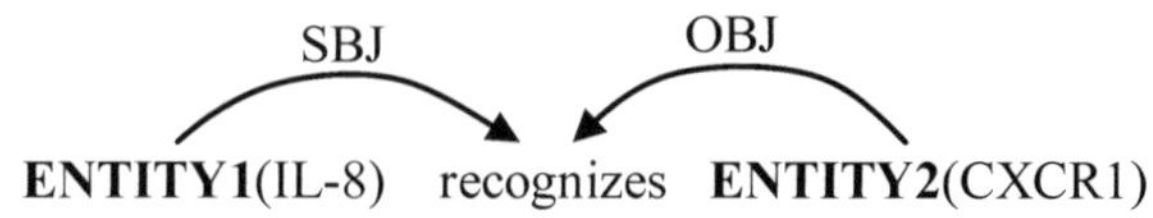

Figure 3: A dependency path between protein names

split, tokenized, and annotated with proteins and PPIs.

4 A data-driven dependency parser for biomedical text

The parser we used as component of our PPI extraction system was a shift-reduce dependency parser that uses maximum entropy models to determine the parser's actions. Our overall parsing approach uses a best-first probabilistic shift-reduce algorithm, working left-to right to find labeled dependencies one at a time. The algorithm is essentially a dependency version of the constituent parsing algorithm for probabilistic parsing with LR-like data-driven models described by Sagae and Lavie (2006). This dependency parser has been shown to have state-of-the-art accuracy in the CoNLL shared tasks on dependency parsing (Buchholz and Marsi, 2006; Nivre, 2007). Sagae and Tsujii (2007) present a detailed description of the parsing approach used in our work, including the parsing algorithm and the features used to classify parser actions. In summary, the parser uses an algorithm similar to the LR parsing algorithm (Knuth, 1965), keeping a stack of partially built syntactic structures, and a queue of remaining input tokens. At each step in the parsing process, the parser can apply a shift action (remove a token from the front of the queue and place it on top of the stack), or a reduce action (pop the two topmost

```
(dep_path (SBJ (ENTITY1 ecognizes))
          (rOBJ (recognizes ENTITY2)))
```

Figure 4: A tree kernel representation of the dependency path

stack items, and push a new item composed of the two popped items combined in a single structure). This parsing approach is very similar to the one used successfully by Nivre et al. (2006), but we use a maximum entropy classifier (Berger et al., 1996) to determine parser actions, which makes parsing considerably faster. In addition, our parsing approach performs a search over the space of possible parser actions, while Nivre et al.'s approach is deterministic.

The parser was trained using 8,000 sentences from the GENIA Treebank (Tateisi et al., 2005), which contains abstracts of papers taken from MEDLINE, annotated with syntactic structures. To determine the effects of training set size on the parser, and consequently on the PPI extraction system, we trained several parsing models with different amounts of GENIA Treebank data. We started with 100 sentences, and increased the training set by 100 sentence increments, up to 1,000 sentences. From that point, we increased the training set by 1,000 sentence increments. Figure 5 shows the labeled dependency accuracy for the varying sizes of training sets. The accuracy was measured on a portion of the GENIA Treebank reserved as development data. The result clearly demonstrates that the increase in the size of the training set contributes to increasing parse accuracy. Training the parser with only 100 sentences results in parse accuracy of about 72.5%. Accuracy rises sharply with additional training data until the size of the training set reaches about 1,000 sentences (about 82.5% accuracy). From there, accuracy climbs consistently, but slowly, until 85.6% accuracy is reached with 8,000 sentences of training data.

It should be noted that parser accuracy on the Aimed data used in our PPI extraction experiments may be slightly lower, since the domain of the GENIA Treebank is not exactly the same as the Aimed corpus. Both of them were extracted from MEDLINE, but the criteria for data selection were not the same in the two corpora, creating possible differences in sub-domains. We also note that the accuracy of a parser trained with more than 40,000 sentences from the Wall Street Journal portion of the Penn Treebank is under 79%, a level equivalent to that obtained by training the parser with only 500 sentences of GENIA data.

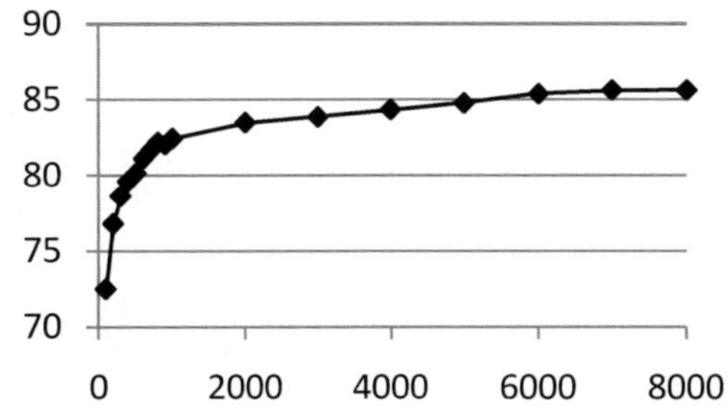

Figure 5: Data size vs. parse accuracy

5 Experiments and Results

In this section we present our PPI extraction experiments applying the dependency parsers trained with the different amounts of the GENIA Treebank in our PPI system. As we mentioned, the GENIA Treebank is used for training the parser, while the Aimed is used for training and evaluation of PPI extraction. A part-of-speech tagger trained with GENIA and PennBioIE was used. We do not apply automatic protein name detection, and instead use the gold-standard protein annotations in the Aimed corpus. Before running a parser, multiword protein names are concatenated and treated as single words. As described in Section 3, bag-of-words and syntactic dependency paths are fed as features to the PPI classifier. The accuracy of PPI extraction is measured by the abstract-wise 10-fold cross validation (Sætre et al, 2007).

When we use the part-of-speech tagger and the dependency parser trained with WSJ, the accuracy (F-score) of PPI extraction on this data set is 55.2. The accuracy increases to 56.9 when we train the part-of-speech tagger with GENIA and Penn BioIE, while using the WSJ-trained parser. This confirms the claims by Lease and Charniak (2005) that subsentential lexical analysis alone is helpful in adapting WSJ parsers to the biomedical domain. While Lease and Charniak looked only at parse accuracy, our result shows that the increase in parse accuracy is, as expected, beneficial in practice.

Figure 6 shows the relationship between the amount of parser training data and the F-score for the PPI extraction. The result shows that the accuracy of PPI extraction increases with the use of more sentences to train the parser. The best accuracy was obtained when using 4,000 sentences, where parsing accuracy is around 84.3. Although it may appear that further increasing the training data for the parser may not improve the PPI extraction accuracy (since only small and inconsistent variations in F-score are observed in Figure 6), when we plot the curves shown in Figures 5 and 6 in a single graph (Figure 7), we see that the two curves match each other to a large extent. This is supported by the strong correlation between parse accuracy and PPI accuracy observed in Figure 8. While this suggests that training the parser with a larger treebank may result in improved accuracy in PPI extraction, we observe that a 1% absolute improvement in parser accuracy corresponds roughly to a 0.25 improvement in PPI extraction F-score. Figure 5 indicates that to obtain even a 1% improvement in parser accuracy by using more training data, the size of the treebank would have to increase significantly.

Although the results presented so far seem to suggest the need for a large data annotation effort to achieve a meaningful improvement in PPI extraction accuracy, there are other ways to improve the overall accuracy of the system without an improvement in parser accuracy. One obvious alternative is to increase the size of the PPI-annotated corpus (which is distinct from the treebank used to train the parser). As mentioned in section 3, our system is trained using the Aimed corpus, which contains 225 abstracts from biomedical papers with manual annotations indicating interactions between proteins. Pairs of proteins with no interaction described in the text are used as negative examples, and pairs of proteins described as interacting are used as positive examples. The corpus contains a total of roughly 9,000 examples. Figure 9 shows how the overall system accuracy varies when different amounts of training data (varying amounts of training examples) are used to train the PPI system (keeping the parse accuracy constant, using all of the available training data in the GENIA treebank to train the parser). While Figure 5 indicates that a significant improvement in parse accuracy requires a large increase in the treebank used to train the parser, and Figure 7 shows that improvements in PPI extraction accuracy may require a sizable improvement in parse accuracy, Figure 9 suggests that even a relatively small increase in the PPI corpus may lead to a significant improvement in PPI extraction accuracy.

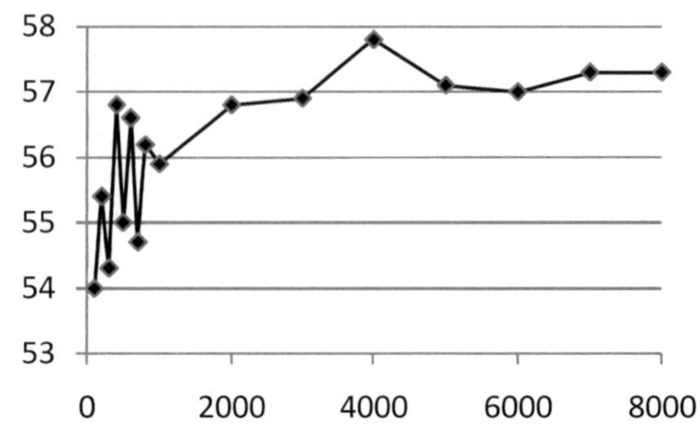

Figure 6: Parser training data size vs. PPI extraction accuracy

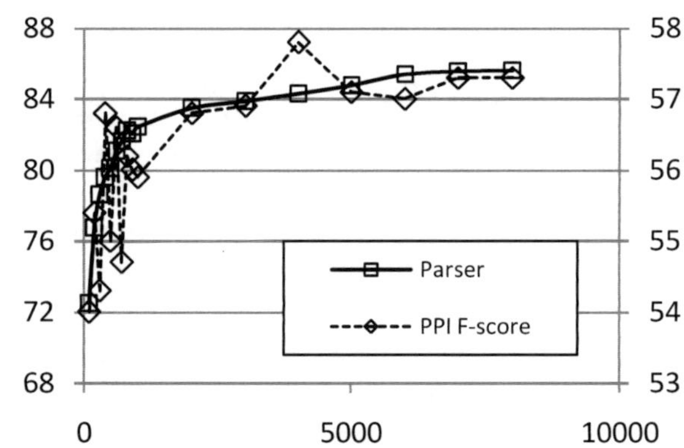

Figure 7: Parser training data size vs. parser accuracy and PPI extraction accuracy

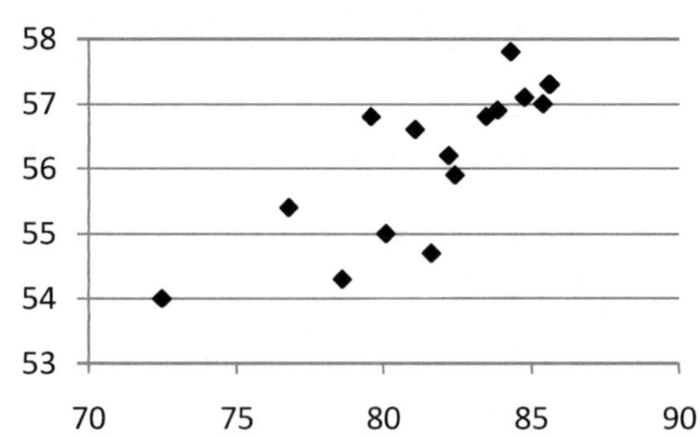

Figure 8: Parse accuracy vs. PPI extraction accuracy

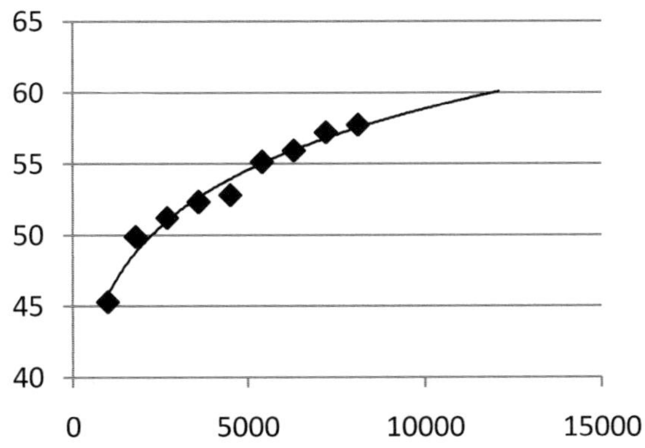

Figure 9: Number of PPI training examples vs. PPI extraction accuracy

While some of the conclusions that can be drawn from these results may be somewhat surprising, most are entirely expected. However, even in these straightforward cases, our experiments provide some empirical evidence and concrete quantitative analysis to complement intuition. We see that using domain-specific training data for the parsing component for the PPI extraction system produces superior results, compared to using training data from the WSJ Penn Treebank. When the parser trained on WSJ sentences is used, PPI extraction accuracy is about 55, compared to over 57 when sentences from biomedical papers are used. This corresponds fairly closely to the differences in parser accuracy: the accuracy of the parser trained on 500 sentences from GENIA is about the same as the accuracy of the parser trained on the entire WSJ Penn Treebank, and when these parsers are used in the PPI extraction system, they result in similar overall task accuracy. However, the results obtained when a domain-specific POS tagger is combined with a parser trained with out-of-domain data, overall PPI results are nearly at the same level as those obtained with domain-specific training data (just below 57 with a domain-specific POS tagger and out-of-domain parser, and just above 57 for domain-specific POS tagger and parser). At the same time, the argument against annotating domain-specific data for parsers in new domains is not a strong one, since higher accuracy levels (for both the parser and the overall system) can be obtained with a relatively small amount of domain-specific data.

Figures 5, 6 and 7 also suggest that additional efforts in improving parser accuracy (through the use of feature engineering, other machine learning techniques, or an increase in the size of its training set) could improve PPI extraction accuracy, but a large improvement in parser accuracy may be required. When we combine these results with the findings obtained by Miyao et al. (2008), they suggest that a better way to improve the overall system is to spend more effort in designing a specific syntactic representation that addresses the needs of the system, instead of using a generic representation designed for measuring parser accuracy. Another potentially fruitful course of action is to design more sophisticated and effective ways for information extraction systems to use NLP tools, rather than simply extracting features that correspond to small fragments of syntactic trees. Of course, making proper use of natural language analysis is a considerable challenge, but one that should be kept in mind through the design of practical systems that use NLP components.

6 Conclusion

This paper presented empirical results on the relationship between the amount of training data used to create a dependency parser, and the accuracy of a system that performs identification of protein-protein interactions using the dependency parser. We trained a dependency parser with different amounts of data from the GENIA Treebank to establish how the improvement in parse accuracy corresponds to improvement in practical task performance in this information extraction task. While parsing accuracy clearly increased with larger amounts of data, and is likely to continue increasing with additional annotation of data for the GENIA Treebank, the trend in the accuracy of PPI extraction indicates that a sizable improvement in parse accuracy may be necessary for improved detection of protein interactions.

When combined with recent findings by Miyao et al. (2008), our results indicate that further work in designing PPI extraction systems that use syntactic dependency features would benefit from more adequate syntactic representations or more sophisticated use of NLP than simple extraction of syntactic subtrees. Furthermore, to improve accuracy in this task, efforts on data annotation should focus on task-specific data (manual annotation of protein interactions in biomedical papers), rather than on additional training data for syntactic parsers. While annotation of parser training data might seems like a cost-effective choice, since improved parser results might be beneficial in a number of systems where the parser can be used, our results show that, in this particular task, efforts should be focused elsewhere, such as the annotation of addition PPI data.

Acknowledgements

We thank the anonymous reviewers for their insightful comments. This work was partially supported by Grant-in-Aid for Specially Promoted Research (MEXT, Japan), Genome Network Project (MEXT, Japan), and Grant-in-Aid for Young Scientists (MEXT, Japan).

References

Berger, A., S. A. Della Pietra, and V. J. Della Pietra. 1996. A maximum entropy approach to natural language processing. *Computational Linguistics*, 22(1):39–71.

Clegg, A. and Shepherd, A. 2007. Benchmarking natural-language parsers for biological applications using dependency graphs. BMC Bioinformatics, 8:24.

Erkan, G., A. Ozgur, and D. R. Radev. 2007. Semisupervised classification for extracting protein interaction sentences using dependency parsing. In *Proceedings of CoNLL-EMNLP 2007.*

Hara, T., Miyao, Y and Tsujii, J. 2007. Evaluating Impact of Re-training a Lexical Disambiguation Model on Domain Adaptation of an HPSG Parser. In *Proceedings of the International Conference on Parsing Technologies (IWPT).*

Katrenko, S. and P. W. Adriaans. 2006. Learning relations from biomedical corpora using dependency trees. In *Proceedings of the first workshop on Knowledge Discovery and Emergent Complexity in BioInformatics (KDECB),* pages 61–80.

Kulick, S., A. Bies, M. Liberman, M. Mandel, R. McDonald, M. Palmer, A. Schein and L. Ungar. 2004. Integrated Annotation for Biomedical Information Extraction. In *Proceedings of Biolink 2004: Linking Biological Literature, Ontologies and Databases (HLT-NAACL workshop).*

Lease, M. and Charniak, E. 2005. Parsing Biomedical Literature. In R. Dale, K.-F. Wong, J. Su, and O. Kwong, editors, *Proceedings of the 2nd International Joint Conference on Natural Language Processing (IJCNLP'05)*, volume 3651 of Lecture Notes in Computer Science, pages 58 – 69.

Miyao, Y., Sætre, R., Sagae, K., Matsuzaki, T. and Tsujii, J. 2008. Task-Oriented Evaluation of Syntactic Parsers and Their Representations. In *Proceedings of the 46th Annual Meeting of the Association for Computational Linguistics.*

Nivre, J., Hall, J., Kubler, S., McDonald, R., Nilsson, J., Riedel, S. and Yuret, D. 2007. The CoNLL 2007 Shared Task on Dependency Parsing. In *Proceedings the CoNLL 2007 Shared Task in EMNLP-CoNLL.*

Nivre, Joakim, Johan Hall, Jens Nilsson, Gulsen Eryigit,and Svetoslav Marinov. 2006. Labeled pseudo-projective dependency parsing with support vector machines. In *Proceedings of the Tenth Conference on Computational Natural Language Learning, shared task session.*

Pyysalo S., Ginter F., Haverinen K., Heimonen J., Salakoski T. and Laippala V. 2007. On the unification of syntactic annotations under the Stanford dependency scheme: A case study on BioInfer and GENIA. In *Proceedings of BioNLP 2007: Biological, Translational and Clinical Language Processing.*

Quirk, C. and Corston-Oliver S. 2006. The impact of parse quality on syntactically-informed statistical machine translation. In *Proceedings of EMNLP 2007.*

Sætre, R., Sagae, K., and Tsujii, J. 2007. Syntactic features for protein-protein interaction extraction. In *Proceedings of the International Symposium on Languages in Biology and Medicine (LBM short oral presentations).*

Sagae, K. and Lavie, A. 2006. A best-first probabilistic shift-reduce parser. In *Proceedings of the COLING/ACL 2006 Main Conference Poster Sessions*, pages 691–698, Sydney, Australia, July. Association for Computational Linguistics.

Sagae, K., Miyao, Y. and Tsujii, J. 2008. Challenges in Mapping of Syntactic Representations for Framework-Independent Parser Evaluation. In *Proceedings of the Workshop on Automated Syntatic Annotations for Interoperable Language Resources at the First International Conference on Global Interoperability for Language Resources (ICGL'08).*

Tateisi, Y., Yakushiji, A., Ohta, T., and Tsujii, J. 2005. Syntax annotation for the GENIA corpus. In *Proceedings Second International Joint Conference on Natural Language Processing: Companion Volume including Posters/Demos and tutorial abstracts.*

Adapting naturally occurring test suites for evaluation of clinical question answering

Dina Demner-Fushman
Lister Hill National Center for Biomedical Communications,
National Library of Medicine, NIH, Bethesda, MD 20894, USA
ddemner@mail.nih.gov

Abstract

This paper describes the structure of a test suite for evaluation of clinical question answering systems; presents several manually compiled resources found useful for test suite generation; and describes the adaptation of these resources for evaluation of a clinical question answering system.

1 Introduction

The community-wide interest in rapid development in many areas of natural language processing and information retrieval resulted in creation of reusable test collections in large-scale evaluations such as the Text REtrieval Conference (TREC)[1]. Researchers in more specific areas, for which no TREC or other collections are available, have to create or find suitable test collections to evaluate their systems.

For example, Cramer et al. (2006) recruited volunteers and quickly gathered a sizeable corpus of question-answer pairs for evaluation of German open-domain question answering systems. This was achieved through a Web-based tool that allowed marking up "interesting" passages in Wikipedia articles and then asking questions about the content of those passages. This appealing approach can not easily be applied in the domain of clinical question answering because the quality of the questions and answers as well as the answer completeness are paramount. A test suite for evaluation of clinical question answering systems should contain a set of real-life questions asked by clinicians and high-quality answers compiled by experts. The answers should be presented in the form deemed useful by clinicians.

One of the benefits of focusing on a specific domain, such as clinical question answering, is that the user-needs and desirable results are well-studied and their descriptions are readily-available. In the case of clinical question answering, clinicians' desiderata are: to see a "bottom-line advice" first, have on-demand access to the context that was used in generation of the advice, and finally have access to the original sources of information (Ely et al., 2005). A fair number of high-quality manually created collections present answers to clinical questions in this form and could be obtained online. Three partially freely-available sources: Family Practitioner Inquiry Network (FPIN)[2], Parkhurst Exchange Forum (PE)[3], and BMJ Clinical Evidence (BMJ-CE)[4] were used to design and develop the presented test suites and evaluation methods.

Although there seems to be a distinction between `test collections` and `test suites` (Cohen et al., 2004) (the former defined as "pieces of text" and associated with corpora, the latter, as lists of specially constructed sentences, or sentence sequences, or sentence fragments (Balkan et al., 1994)), evaluation of answers to clinical questions crosses this boundary and requires the availability of carefully generated sentence fragments as well as suitable document collections.

[1] http://trec.nist.gov/

[2] http://www.primeanswers.org/primeanswers/

[3] http://www.parkhurstexchange.com/qa/index.php

[4] http://www.clinicalevidence.com/ceweb/conditions/index.jsp

Software Engineering, Testing, and Quality Assurance for Natural Language Processing, pages 21–22,
Columbus, Ohio, USA, June 2008. ©2008 Association for Computational Linguistics

2 Test suite structure

The multi-tiered answer model of the FPIN and BMJ-CE resources is adapted in this work. The top tier contains the "bottom-line advice". FPIN provides the key-points of the advice in the form of a short sentence sequence, whereas BMJ-CE provides a list of sentence fragments (see Figure 1). Both sources employ experts in question areas to carefully construct the answers. The second tier elaborates each of the key-points in 2-3 paragraph-long summaries generated by the same experts. The third tier provides references to the original sources used in answer compilation.

Likely to be beneficial:

- Angiotensin converting enzyme inhibitors
- Aspirin
- β Blockers ...

Trade-off between benefits and harms:

- Nitrates (in the absence of thrombolysis)

Likely to be ineffective or harmful: ...

Figure 1: The top tier of a multi-tiered answer to the clinical question *How to improve outcomes in acute myocardial infarction?* contains key-points generated by a panel of cardiologists.

3 Using the test suite in an evaluation

The answer presented in Figure 1 can be used to evaluate a system's answer to this question by extracting the reference list from the FPIN or BMJ-CE answer. Similarly, the second-tier summaries can be used to evaluate the context for the key-points generated by a system. The references can be used to evaluate the quality of the original sources retrieved by a system if the documents in both lists are represented using their unique identifiers: DOI or a PubMed[5] identifier. Availability of these test suites provides for the following evaluation forms:

- diagnostic, in which developers could evaluate how a tier is affected by changes in its own module(s) or in the underlying tiers;
- task-oriented, in which the system is evaluated as a whole on its ability to answer clinical questions.

It is conceivable to evaluate a system as a whole by evaluating its performance in each tier and then combining the results. In a task-oriented evaluation, it seems reasonable to evaluate the quality of the first-tier answer and verify the adequacy of the second-tier context.

3.1 Caveats

Even the simplest case of the top-tier evaluation, checking the list of fragments generated by a system against the reference list, ideally should be conducted manually by a person with biomedical background. For example, *Acetylsalicylic acid* in a system's answer needs to be matched to *Aspirin* in the reference list. Automation of this step is possible through mapping of both lists to an ontology, e.g., UMLS[6], but such evaluation will be significantly less accurate and potentially biased (if a system uses the same mapping algorithm to find the answer).

A manual evaluation based on 30 of 54 BMJ-CE question-answer pairs in the presented test suite is described in (Demner-Fushman and Lin, 2006). Another 50 question-answer pairs originated in FPIN and PE.

References

Cramer I., Leidner J.L. and Klakow D. 2006. Building an Evaluation Corpus for German Question Answering by Harvesting Wikipedia. *LREC-2006*, Genoa, Italy.

Cohen K.B., Tanabe L., Kinoshita S., and Hunter L. 2004. A resource for constructing customized test suites for molecular biology entity identification systems. *HLT-NAACL 2004 Workshop: Biolink 2004*, Boston, Massachusetts

Balkan L., Netter K., Arnold D. and Meijer S. 1994. TSNLP. Test Suites for Natural Language Processing. *Language Engineering Convention*, Paris, France.

Ely J.W., Osheroff J.A., Chambliss M.L., Ebell M.H. and Rosenbaum M.E. 2005. Answering Physicians' Clinical Questions: Obstacles and Potential Solutions. *JAMIA*, 12(2):217–224.

Demner-Fushman D. and Lin J. 2006. Answer Extraction, Semantic Clustering, and Extractive Summarization for Clinical Question Answering. *ACL 2006*, Sydney, Australia

[5] http://www.ncbi.nlm.nih.gov/sites/entrez

[6] http://www.nlm.nih.gov/research/umls/

Software testing and the naturally occurring data assumption in natural language processing*

K. Bretonnel Cohen **William A. Baumgartner, Jr.** **Lawrence Hunter**

Abstract

It is a widely accepted belief in natural language processing research that naturally occurring data is the best (and perhaps the only appropriate) data for testing text mining systems. This paper compares code coverage using a suite of functional tests and using a large corpus and finds that higher class, line, and branch coverage is achieved with structured tests than with even a very large corpus.

1 Introduction

In 2006, Geoffrey Chang was a star of the protein crystallography world. That year, a crucial component of his code was discovered to have a simple error with large consequences for his research. The nature of the bug was to change the signs (positive versus negative) of two columns of the output. The effect of this was to reverse the predicted "handedness" of the structure of the molecule—an important feature in predicting its interactions with other molecules. The protein for his work on which Chang was best known is an important one in predicting things like human response to anticancer drugs and the likelihood of bacteria developing antibiotic resistance, so his work was quite influential and heavily cited. The consequences for Chang were the withdrawal of 5 papers in some of the most prestigious journals in the world. The consequences for the rest of the scientific community have not been quantified, but were substantial: prior to the retractions, publishing papers with results that did not jibe with his model's predictions was difficult, and obtaining grants based on preliminary results that seemed to contradict his published results was difficult as well. The Chang story (for a succinct discussion, see (Miller, 2006), and see (Chang et al., 2006) for the retractions) is an object illustration of the truth of Rob Knight's observation that "For scientific work, bugs don't just mean unhappy users who you'll never actually meet: they mean retracted publications and ended careers. It is critical that your code be fully tested before you draw conclusions from results it produces" (personal communication). Nonetheless, the subject of software testing has been largely neglected in academic natural language processing. This paper addresses one aspect of software testing: the monitoring of testing efforts via code coverage.

1.1 Code coverage

Code coverage is a numerical assessment of the amount of code that is executed during the running of a test suite (McConnell, 2004). Although it is by no means a completely sufficient method for determining the completeness of a testing effort, it is nonetheless a helpful member of any suite of metrics for assessing testing effort completeness. Code coverage is a metric in the range 0-1.0. A value of 0.86 indicates that 86% of the code was executed while running a given test suite. 100% coverage is difficult to achieve for any nontrivial application, but in general, high degrees of "uncovered" code should lead one to suspect that there is a large amount of

*K. Bretonnel Cohen is with The MITRE Corporation. All three co-authors are at the Center for Computational Pharmacology in the University of Colorado School of Medicine.

Software Engineering, Testing, and Quality Assurance for Natural Language Processing, pages 23–30, Columbus, Ohio, USA, June 2008. ©2008 Association for Computational Linguistics

code that might harbor undetected bugs simply due to never having been executed. A variety of code coverage metrics exist. *Line coverage* indicates the proportion of lines of code that have been executed. It is not the most revealing form of coverage assessment (Kaner et al., 1999, p. 43), but is a basic part of any coverage measurement assessment. *Branch coverage* indicates the proportion of branches within conditionals that have been traversed (Marick, 1997, p. 145). For example, for the conditional `if $a && $b`, there are two possible branches—one is traversed if the expression evaluates to `true`, and the other if it evaluates to `false`. It is more informative than line coverage. *Logic coverage* (also known as *multicondition coverage* (Myers, 1979) and *condition coverage* (Kaner et al., 1999, p. 44) indicates the proportion of sets of variable values that have been tried—a superset of the possible branches traversed. For example, for the conditional `if $a || $b`, the possible cases (assuming no short-circuit logic) are those of the standard (logical) truth table for that conditional. These coverage types are progressively more informative than line coverage. Other types of coverage are less informative than line coverage. For example, *function coverage* indicates the proportion of functions that are called. There is no guarantee that each line in a called function is executed, and all the more so no guarantee that branch or logic coverage is achieved within it, so this type of coverage is weaker than line coverage. With the advent of object-oriented programming, function coverage is sometimes replaced by *class coverage*—a measure of the number of classes that are covered.

We emphasize again that code coverage is not a sufficient metric for evaluating testing completeness in isolation—for example, it is by definition unable to detect "errors of omission," or bugs that consist of a failure to implement needed functionality. Nonetheless, it remains a useful part of a larger suite of metrics, and one study found that testing in the absence of concurrent assessment of code coverage typically results in only 50-60% of the code being executed ((McConnell, 2004, p. 526), citing Wiegers 2002).

We set out to question whether a dominant, if often unspoken, assumption of much work in contemporary NLP holds true: that feeding a program a large corpus serves to exercise it adequately. We began with an information extraction application that had been built for us by a series of contractors, with the contractors receiving constant remote oversight and guidance but without ongoing monitoring of the actual code-writing. The application had benefitted from no testing other than that done by the developers. We used a sort of "translucent-box" or "gray-box" paradigm, meaning in this case that we treated the program under test essentially as a black box whose internals were inaccessible to us, but with the exception that we inserted hooks to a coverage tool. We then monitored three types of coverage—line coverage, branch coverage, and class coverage—under a variety of contrasting conditions:

- A set of developer-written functional tests versus a large corpus with a set of semantic rules optimized for that corpus.
- Varying the size of the rule set.
- Varying the size of the corpus.

We then looked for coverage differences between the various combinations of input data and rule sets. In this case, the null hypothesis is that no differences would be observed. In contrast with the null hypothesis, the unspoken assumption in much NLP work is that the null hypothesis does not hold, that the primary determinant of coverage will be the size of the corpus, and that the observed pattern will be that coverage is higher with the large corpus than when the input is not a large corpus.

2 Methods and materials

2.1 The application under test

The application under test was an information extraction application known as OpenDMAP. It is described in detail in (Hunter et al., 2008). It achieved the highest performance on one measure of the protein-protein interaction task in the BioCreative II shared task (Krallinger et al., 2007). Its use in that task is described specifically in (Baumgartner Jr. et al., In press). It contains 7,024 lines of code spread across three packages (see Table 1). One major package deals with representing the semantic grammar rules themselves, while the other deals with applying the rules to and extracting data from arbitrary textual input. (A minor package deals with

Component	Lines of code
Parser	3,982
Rule-handling	2,311
Configuration	731
Total	7,024

Table 1: Distribution of lines of code in the application.

the configuration files and is mostly not discussed in this paper.)

The rules and patterns that the system uses are typical "semantic grammar" rules in that they allow the free mixing of literals and non-terminals, with the non-terminals typically representing domain-specific types such as "protein interaction verb." Non-terminals are represented as classes. Those classes are defined in a Protégé ontology. Rules typically contain at least one element known as a *slot*. Slot-fillers can be constrained by classes in the ontology. Input that matches a slot is extracted as one of the participants in a relation. A limited regular expression language can operate over classes, literals, or slots. The following is a representative rule. Square brackets indicate slots, curly braces indicate a class, the question-mark is a regular expression operator, and any other text is a literal.

```
{c-interact} := [interactor1]
{c-interact-verb} the?
[interactor2]
```

The input *NEF binds PACS-2* (PMID 18296443) would match that rule. The result would be the recognition of a protein interaction event, with interactor1 being *NEF* and interactor2 being *PACS-2*. Not all rules utilize all possibilities of the rule language, and we took this into account in one of our experiments; we discuss the rules further later in the paper in the context of that experiment.

2.2 Materials

In this work, we made use of the following sets of materials.

- A large data set distributed as training data for part of the BioCreative II shared task. It is described in detail in (Krallinger et al., 2007). Briefly, its domain is molecular biology, and in particular protein-protein interactions—an important topic of research in computational bioscience, with significance to a wide range of topics in biology, including understanding the mechanisms of human diseases (Kann et al., 2006). The corpus contained 3,947,200 words, making it almost an order of magnitude larger than the most commonly used biomedical corpus (GENIA, at about 433K words). This data set is publicly available via `biocreative.sourceforge.net`.

- In conjunction with that data set: a set of 98 rules written in a data-driven fashion by manually examining the BioCreative II data described just above. These rules were used in the BioCreative II shared task, where they achieved the highest score in one category. The set of rules is available on our SourceForge site at `bionlp.sourceforge.net`.

- A set of functional tests created by the primary developer of the system. Table 2 describes the breakdown of the functional tests across various aspects of the design and functionality of the application.

Test type	Number of tests
Basic	85
Pattern/rule	67
Patterns only	90
Slots	9
Slot nesting	7
Slot property	20
Total	278

Table 2: Distribution of functional tests.

2.3 Assessing coverage

We used the open-source Cobertura tool (Mark Doliner, personal communication; `cobertura.sourceforge.net`) to measure coverage. Cobertura reports line coverage and branch coverage on a per-package basis and, within each package, on a per-class basis[1].

The architecture of the application is such that Cobertura's per-package approach resulted in three

[1]Cobertura is Java-specific. PyDEV provides code coverage analysis for Python, as does Coverage.py.

sets of coverage reports: for the configuration file processing code, for the rule-processing code, and for the parser code. We report results for the application as a whole, for the parser code, and for the rule-processing code. We did note differences in the configuration code coverage for the various conditions, but it does not change the overall conclusions of the paper and is omitted from most of the discussion due to considerations of space and of general interest.

3 Results

We conducted three separate experiments.

3.1 The most basic experiment: test suite versus corpus

In the most basic experiment, we contrasted class, line, and branch coverage when running the developer-constructed test suite and when running the corpus and the corpus-based rules. Tables 3 and 4 show the resulting data. As the first two lines of Table 3 show, for the entire application (parser, rule-handling, and configuration), line coverage was higher with the test suite—56% versus 41%—and branch coverage was higher as well—41% versus 28% (see the first two lines of Table 3).

We give here a more detailed discussion of the results for the entire code base. (Detailed discussions for the parser and rule packages, including granular assessments of class coverage, follow.)

For the parser package:

- Class coverage was higher with the test suite than with the corpus—88% (22/25) versus 80% (20/25).
- For the entire parser package, line coverage was higher with the test suite than with the corpus—55% versus 41%.
- For the entire parser package, branch coverage was higher with the test suite than with the corpus—57% versus 29%.

Table 4 gives class-level data for the two main packages. For the parser package:

- Within the 25 individual classes of the parser package, line coverage was equal or greater with the test suite for 21/25 classes; it was not just equal but greater for 14/25 classes.
- Within those 21 of the 25 individual classes that had branching logic, branch coverage was equal or greater with the test suite for 19/21 classes, and not just equal but greater for 18/21 classes.

For the rule-handling package:

- Class coverage was higher with the test suite than with the corpus—100% (20/20) versus 90% (18/20).
- For the entire rules package, line coverage was higher with the test suite than with the corpus—63% versus 42%.
- For the entire rules package, branch coverage was higher with the test suite than with the corpus—71% versus 24%.

Table 4 gives the class-level data for the rules package:

- Within the 20 individual classes of the rules package, line coverage was equal or greater with the test suite for 19/20 classes, and not just equal but greater for 6/20 classes.
- Within those 11 of the 20 individual classes that had branching logic, branch coverage was equal or greater with the test suite for all 11/11 classes, and not just equal but greater for (again) all 11/11 classes.

3.2 The second experiment: Varying the size of the rule set

Pilot studies suggested (as later experiments verified) that the size of the input corpus had a negligible effect on coverage. This suggested that it would be worthwhile to assess the effect of the rule set on coverage independently. We used simple ablation (deletion of portions of the rule set) to vary the size of the rule set.

We created two versions of the original rule set. We focussed only on the non-lexical, relational pattern rules, since they are completely dependent on the lexical rules. Each version was about half the

Metric	Functional tests	Corpus, all rules	nominal rules	verbal rules
Overall line coverage	**56%**	41%	41%	41%
Overall branch coverage	**41%**	28%	28%	28%
Parser line coverage	**55%**	41%	41%	41%
Parser branch coverage	**57%**	29%	29%	29%
Rules line coverage	**63%**	42%	42%	42%
Rules branch coverage	**71%**	24%	24%	24%
Parser class coverage	**88%** (22/25)	80% (20/25)		
Rules class coverage	**100%** (20/20)	90% (18/20)		

Table 3: Application and package-level coverage statistics using the developer's functional tests, the full corpus with the full set of rules, and the full corpus with two reduced sets of rules. The highest value in a row is bolded. The final three columns are intentionally identical (see explanation in text).

Package	Line coverage >=	Line coverage >	Branch coverage >=	Branch coverage >
Classes in parser package	21/25	14/25	19/21	18/21
Classes in rules package	19/20	6/20	11/11	11/11

Table 4: When individual classes were examined, both line and branch coverage were always higher with the functional tests than with the corpus. This table shows the magnitude of the differences. >= indicates the number of classes that had equal or greater coverage with the functional tests than with the corpus, and > indicates just the classes that had greater coverage with the functional tests than with the corpus.

size of the original set. The first consisted of the first half of the rule set, which happened to consist primarily of verb-based patterns. The second consisted of the second half of the rule set, which corresponded roughly to the nominalization rules.

The last two columns of Table 3 show the package-level results. Overall, on a per-package basis, there were no differences in line or branch coverage when the data was run against the full rule set or either half of the rule set. (The identity of the last three columns is due to this lack of difference in results between the full rule set and the two reduced rule sets.) On a per-class level, we did note minor differences, but as Table 3 shows, they were within rounding error on the package level.

3.3 The third experiment: Coverage closure

In the third experiment, we looked at how coverage varies as increasingly larger amounts of the corpus are processed. This methodology is comparable to examining the closure properties of a corpus in a corpus linguistics study (see e.g. Chapter 6 of (McEnery and Wilson, 2001)) (and as such may be sensitive to the extent to which the contents of the corpus do or do not fit the sublanguage model). We counted cumulative line coverage as increasingly large amounts of the corpus were processed, ranging from 0 to 100% of its contents. The results for line coverage are shown in Figure 1. (The results for branch coverage are quite similar, and the graph is not shown.) Line coverage for the entire application is indicated by the thick solid line. Line coverage for the parser package is indicated by the thin solid line. Line coverage for the rules package is indicated by the light gray solid line. The broken line indicates the number of pattern matches—quantities should be read off of the right y axis.

The figure shows quite graphically the lack of effect on coverage of increasing the size of the corpus. For the entire application, the line coverage is 27% when an empty document has been read in, and 39% when a single sentence has been processed; it increases by one to 40% when 51 sentences have been processed, and has grown as high as it ever will—41%—by the time 1,000 sentences have been processed. Coverage at 191,478 sentences—that is, 3,947,200 words—is no higher than at 1,000 sentences, and barely higher, percentagewise, than at a single sentence.

An especially notable pattern is that the huge rise

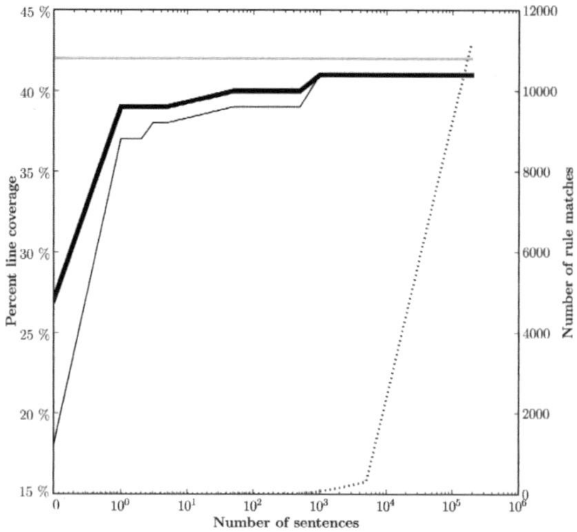

Figure 1: Increase in percentage of line coverage as increasing amounts of the corpus are processed. Left *y* axis is the percent coverage. The *x* axis is the number of sentences. Right *y* axis (scale 0-12,000) is the number of rule matches. The heavy solid line is coverage for the entire package, the thin solid line is coverage for the parser package, the light gray line is coverage for the rules package, and the broken line is the number of pattern matches.

in the number of matches to the rules (graphed by the broken line) between 5,000 sentences and 191K sentences has absolutely no effect on code coverage.

4 Discussion

The null hypothesis—that a synthetic test suite and a naturalistic corpus provide the same code coverage—is not supported by the data shown here. Furthermore, the widely, if implicitly, held assumption that a corpus would provide the best testing data can be rejected, as well. The results reported here are consistent with the hypothesis that code coverage for this application is not affected by the size of the corpus or by the size of the rule set, and that running it on a large corpus does not guarantee thorough testing. Rather, coverage is optimized by traditional software testing.

4.1 Related work

Although software testing is a first-class research object in computer science, it has received little attention in the natural language processing arena. A notable exception to this comes from the grammar engineering community. This has produced a body of publications that includes Oepen's work on test suite design (Oepen et al., 1998), Volk's work on test suite encoding (Volk, 1998), Oepen et al.'s work on the Redwoods project (Oepen et al., 2002), Butt and King's discussion of the importance of testing (Butt and King, 2003), Flickinger et al.'s work on "semantics debugging" with Redwoods data (Flickinger et al., 2005), and Bender et al.'s recent work on test suite generation (Bender et al., 2007). Outside of the realm of grammar engineering, work on testing for NLP is quite limited. (Cohen et al., 2004) describes a methodology for generating test suites for molecular biology named entity recognition systems, and (Johnson et al., 2007) describes the development of a fault model for linguistically-based ontology mapping, alignment, and linking systems. However, when most researchers in the NLP community refer in print to "testing," they do not mean it in the sense in which that term is used in software engineering. Some projects have publicized aspects of their testing work, but have not published on their approaches: the NLTK project posts module-level line coverage statistics, having achieved median coverage of 55% on 116 Python modules[2] and 38% coverage for the project as a whole; the MALLET project indicates on its web site that it encourages the production of unit tests during development, but unfortunately does not go into details of their recommendations for unit-testing machine learning code[3].

4.2 Conclusions

We note a number of shortcomings of code coverage. For example, poor coding conventions can actually inflate your line coverage. Consider a hypothetical application consisting only of the following, written as a single line of code with no line breaks: `if (myVariable == 1) doSomething elsif (myVariable == 2) doSomethingElse elsif (myVariable = 3) doYetAnotherThing` and a poor test suite consisting only of inputs that will cause `myVariable` to ever have the value `1`. The test suite will achieve 100% line coverage for

[2] `nltk.org/doc/guides/coverage`

[3] `mallet.cs.umass.edu/index.php/Guidelines_for_writing_unit_tests`

this application—and without even finding the error that sets `myVariable` to 3 if it is not valued 1 or 2. If the code were written with reasonable line breaks, code coverage would be only 20%. And, as has been noted by others, code coverage can not detect "sins of omission"—bugs that consist of the failure to write needed code (e.g. for error-handling or for input validation). We do not claim that code coverage is wholly sufficient for evaluating a test suite; nonetheless, it is one of a number of metrics that are helpful in judging the adequacy of a testing effort. Another very valuable one is the *found/fixed* or *open/closed graph* (Black, 1999; Baumgartner Jr. et al., 2007).

While remaining aware of the potential shortcomings of code coverage, we also note that the data reported here supports its utility. The developer-written functional tests were produced without monitoring code coverage; even though those tests routinely produced higher coverage than a large corpus of naturalistic text, *they achieved less than 60% coverage overall,* as predicted by Wiegers's work cited in the introduction. We now have the opportunity to raise that coverage via structured testing performed by someone other than the developer. In fact, our first attempts to test the previously unexercised code immediately uncovered two showstopper bugs; the coverage analysis also led us to the discovery that the application's error-handling code was essentially untested.

Although we have explored a number of dimensions of the space of the coverage phenomenon, additional work could be done. We used a relatively naive approach to rule ablation in the second experiment; a more sophisticated approach would be to ablate specific types of rules—for example, ones that do or don't contain slots, ones that do or don't contain regular expression operators, etc.—and monitor the coverage changes. (We did run all three experiments on a separate, smaller corpus as a pilot study; we report the results for the BioCreative II data set in this paper since that is the data for which the rules were optimized. Results in the pilot study were entirely comparable.)

In conclusion: natural language processing applications are particularly susceptible to emergent phenomena, such as interactions between the contents of a rule set and the contents of a corpus. These are especially difficult to control when the evaluation corpus is naturalistic and the rule set is data-driven. Structured testing does not eliminate this emergent nature of the problem space, but it *does* allow for controlled evaluation of the performance of your system. Corpora also are valuable evaluation resources: the *combination* of a structured test suite and a naturalistic corpus provides a powerful set of tools for finding bugs in NLP applications.

Acknowledgments

The authors thank James Firby, who wrote the functional tests, and Helen L. Johnson, who wrote the rules that were used for the BioCreative data. Steve Bethard and Aaron Cohen recommended Python coverage tools. We also thank the three anonymous reviewers.

References

William A. Baumgartner Jr., K. Bretonnel Cohen, Lynne Fox, George K. Acquaah-Mensah, and Lawrence Hunter. 2007. Manual curation is not sufficient for annotation of genomic databases. *Bioinformatics*, 23:i41–i48.

William A. Baumgartner Jr., Zhiyong Lu, Helen L. Johnson, J. Gregory Caporaso, Jesse Paquette, Anna Lindemann, Elizabeth K. White, Olga Medvedeva, K. Bretonnel Cohen, and Lawrence Hunter. In press. Concept recognition for extracting protein interaction relations from biomedical text. *Genome Biology*.

Emily M. Bender, Laurie Poulson, Scott Drellishak, and Chris Evans. 2007. Validation and regression testing for a cross-linguistic grammar resource. In *ACL 2007 Workshop on Deep Linguistic Processing*, pages 136–143, Prague, Czech Republic, June. Association for Computational Linguistics.

Rex Black. 1999. *Managing the Testing Process*.

Miriam Butt and Tracy Holloway King. 2003. Grammar writing, testing and evaluation. In Ali Farghaly, editor, *A handbook for language engineers*, pages 129–179. CSLI.

Geoffrey Chang, Christopher R. Roth, Christopher L. Reyes, Owen Pornillos, Yen-Ju Chen, and Andy P. Chen. 2006. Letters: Retraction. *Science*, 314:1875.

K. Bretonnel Cohen, Lorraine Tanabe, Shuhei Kinoshita, and Lawrence Hunter. 2004. A resource for constructing customized test suites for molecular biology entity identification systems. In *HLT-NAACL 2004 Workshop: BioLINK 2004, Linking Biological Literature, Ontologies and Databases*, pages 1–8. Association for Computational Linguistics.

Dan Flickinger, Alexander Koller, and Stefan Thater. 2005. A new well-formedness criterion for semantics debugging. In *Proceedings of the HPSG05 Conference*.

Lawrence Hunter, Zhiyong Lu, James Firby, William A. Baumgartner Jr., Helen L. Johnson, Philip V. Ogren, and K. Bretonnel Cohen. 2008. OpenDMAP: An open-source, ontology-driven concept analysis engine, with applications to capturing knowledge regarding protein transport, protein interactions and cell-specific gene expression. *BMC Bioinformatics*, 9(78).

Helen L. Johnson, K. Bretonnel Cohen, and Lawrence Hunter. 2007. A fault model for ontology mapping, alignment, and linking systems. In *Pacific Symposium on Biocomputing*, pages 233–244. World Scientific Publishing Company.

Cem Kaner, Hung Quoc Nguyen, and Jack Falk. 1999. *Testing computer software, 2nd edition*. John Wiley and Sons.

Maricel Kann, Yanay Ofran, Marco Punta, and Predrag Radivojac. 2006. Protein interactions and disease. In *Pacific Symposium on Biocomputing*, pages 351–353. World Scientific Publishing Company.

Martin Krallinger, Florian Leitner, and Alfonso Valencia. 2007. Assessment of the second BioCreative PPI task: automatic extraction of protein-protein interactions. In *Proceedings of the Second BioCreative Challenge Evaluation Workshop*.

Brian Marick. 1997. *The craft of software testing: subsystem testing including object-based and object-oriented testing*. Prentice Hall.

Steve McConnell. 2004. *Code complete*. Microsoft Press, 2nd edition.

Tony McEnery and Andrew Wilson. 2001. *Corpus Linguistics*. Edinburgh University Press, 2nd edition.

Greg Miller. 2006. A scientist's nightmare: software problem leads to five retractions. *Science*, 314:1856–1857.

Glenford Myers. 1979. *The art of software testing*. John Wiley and Sons.

S. Oepen, K. Netter, and J. Klein. 1998. TSNLP - test suites for natural language processing. In John Nerbonne, editor, *Linguistic Databases*, chapter 2, pages 13–36. CSLI Publications.

Stephan Oepen, Kristina Toutanova, Stuart Shieber, Christopher Manning, Dan Flickinger, and Thorsten Brants. 2002. The LinGO Redwoods treebank: motivation and preliminary applications. In *Proceedings of the 19th international conference on computational linguistics*, volume 2.

Martin Volk. 1998. Markup of a test suite with SGML. In John Nerbonne, editor, *Linguistic databases*, pages 59–76. CSLI Publications.

Building a BioWordNet by Using WordNet's Data Formats and WordNet's Software Infrastructure — A Failure Story

Michael Poprat **Elena Beisswanger** **Udo Hahn**

Jena University Language & Information Engineering (JULIE) Lab
Friedrich-Schiller-Universität Jena
D-07743 Jena, Germany
{poprat,beisswanger,hahn}@coling-uni-jena.de

Abstract

In this paper, we describe our efforts to build on WordNet resources, using WordNet lexical data, the data format that it comes with and WordNet's software infrastructure in order to generate a biomedical extension of WordNet, the BioWordNet. We began our efforts on the assumption that the software resources were stable and reliable. In the course of our work, it turned out that this belief was far too optimistic. We discuss the stumbling blocks that we encountered, point out an error in the WordNet software with implications for research based on it, and conclude that building on the legacy of WordNet data structures and its associated software might preclude sustainable extensions that go beyond the domain of general English.

1 Introduction

WordNet (Fellbaum, 1998) is one of the most authoritative lexical resources for the general English language. Due to its coverage – currently more than 150,000 lexical items – and its lexicological richness in terms of definitions (glosses) and semantic relations, synonymy via synsets in particular, it has become a *de facto* standard for all sorts of research that rely on lexical content for the English language.

Besides this perspective on rich lexicological data, over the years a software infrastructure has emerged around WordNet that was equally approved by the NLP community. This included, e.g., a lexicographic file generator, various editors and visualization tools but also meta tools relying on properly formated WordNet data such as a library of similarity measures (Pedersen et al., 2004). In numerous articles the usefulness of this data and software ensemble has been demonstrated (e.g., for word sense disambiguation (Patwardhan et al., 2003), the analysis of noun phrase conjuncts (Hogan, 2007), or the resolution of coreferences (Harabagiu et al., 2001)).

In our research on information extraction and text mining within the field of biomedical NLP, we similarly recognized an urgent need for a lexical resource comparable to WordNet, both in scope and size. However, the direct usability of the original WordNet for biomedical NLP is severely hampered by a (not so surprising) lack of coverage of the life sciences domain in the general-language English WordNet as was clearly demonstrated by Burgun and Bodenreider (2001).

Rather than building a BioWordNet by hand, as was done for the general-language English WordNet, our idea to set up a WordNet-style lexical resource for the life sciences was different. We wanted to *link* the original WordNet with various biomedical terminological resources vastly available in the life sciences domain. As an obvious candidate for this merger, we chose one of the major high-coverage umbrella systems for biomedical ontologies, the Open Biomedical Ontologies (OBO).[1] These (currently) over 60 OBO ontologies provide domain-specific knowledge in terms of hierarchies of classes that often come with synonyms and textual definitions for lots of biomedical subdomains (such as genes, proteins, cells, sequences,

[1] http://www.bioontology.org/repositories.html#obo

Software Engineering, Testing, and Quality Assurance for Natural Language Processing, pages 31–39,
Columbus, Ohio, USA, June 2008. ©2008 Association for Computational Linguistics

etc.).[2] Given these resources and their software infrastructure, our plan was to create a biomedically focused lexicological resource, the BIOWORDNET, whose coverage would exceed that of any of its component resources in a so far unprecedented manner. Only then, given such a huge combined resource advanced NLP tasks such as anaphora resolution seem likely to be tackled in a feasible way (Hahn et al., 1999; Castaño et al., 2002; Poprat and Hahn, 2007). In particular, we wanted to make *direct* use of available software infrastructure such as the library of similarity metrics without the need for re-programming and hence foster the reuse of existing software *as is*.

We began our efforts on the assumption that the WORDNET software resources were stable and reliable. In the course of our work, it turned out that this belief was far too optimistic. We discuss the stumbling blocks that we encountered, point out an error in the WORDNET software with implications for research based on it, and conclude that building on the legacy of WORDNET data structures and its associated software might preclude sustainable extensions that go beyond the domain of general English. Hence, our report contains one of the rare failure stories (not only) in our field.

2 Software Around WORDNET Data

While the stock of lexical data assembled in the WORDNET lexicon was continuously growing over time,[3] its data format and storage structures, the so-called *lexicographic file*, by and large, remained unaltered (see Section 2.1). In Section 2.2, we will deal with two important software components with which the lexicographic file can be created and browsed. Over the years, together with the continuous extension of the WORDNET lexicon, a lot of software tools have been developed in various programming languages allowing browsing and accessing WORDNET as well as calculating semantic similarities on it. We will discuss the most relevant of these tools in Section 2.3.

[2] Bodenreider and Burgun (2002) point out that the structure of definitions in WORDNET differ to some degree from more domain-specialized sources such as medical dictionaries.

[3] The latest version 3.0 was released in December 2006

2.1 Lexicon Organization of WORDNET and Storage in Lexicographic Files

At the top level, WORDNET is organized according to four parts of speech, *viz.* noun, verb, adjective and adverb. The most recent version 3.0 covers more than 117,000 nouns, 11,500 verbs, 21,400 adjectives and 4,400 adverbs, interlinked by *lexical relations*, mostly derivations. The basic semantic unit for all parts of speech are sets of synonymous words, so-called *synsets*. These are connected by different semantic relations, imposing a thesaurus-like structure on WORDNET. In this paper, we discuss the organization of noun synsets in WORDNET only, because this is the relevant part of WORDNET for our work. There are two important *semantic* relation types linking noun synsets. The *hypernym / hyponym* relation on which the whole WORDNET noun sense hierarchy is built links more specific to more general synsets, while the *meronym / holonym* relation describes partonomic relations between synsets, such as part of the whole, member of the whole or substance of the whole.

From its very beginning, WORDNET was built and curated manually. Lexicon developing experts introduced new lexical entries into WORDNET, grouped them into synsets and defined appropriate semantic and lexical relations. Since WORDNET was intended to be an electronic lexicon, a data representation format had to be defined as well. When the WORDNET project started more than two decades ago, markup languages such as SGML or XML were unknown. Because of this reason, a rather idiosyncratic, fully text-based data structure for these lexicographic files was defined in a way to be readable and editable by humans — and survived until to-day. This can really be considered as an outdated legacy given the fact that the WORDNET community has been so active in the last years in terms of data collection, but has refrained from adapting its data formats in a comparable way to to-day's specification standards. Very basically,[4] each line in the lexicographic file holds one synset that is enclosed by curly brackets. Take as an example the synset for "monkey":

[4] A detailed description can be found in the WORDNET manual *wninput(5WN)*, available from `http://wordnet.princeton.edu/man/wninput.5WN`.

```
{ monkey, primate,@ (any of various
long-tailed primates (excluding the
prosimians)) }
```

Within the brackets at the first position synonyms are listed, separated by commas. In the example, there is only one synonym, namely "monkey". The synonyms are followed by semantic relations to other synsets, if available. In the example, there is only one hypernym relation (denoted by "@") pointing to the synset "primate". The final position is reserved for the gloss of the synset encapsulated in round brackets. It is important to notice that there are no identifiers for synsets in the lexicographic file. Rather, the string expressions themselves serve as identifiers. Given the fundamental idea of synsets – all words within a synset mean exactly the same in a certain context – it is sufficient to relate one word in the synset in order to refer to the whole synset. Still, there must be a way to deal with homonyms, i.e., lexical items which share the same string, but have different meanings. WORDNET's approach to distinguish different senses of a word is to add numbers from 0 to 15, called *lexical identifiers*. Hence, in WORDNET, a word cannot be more than 16-fold ambiguous. This must be kept in mind when one wants to build a WORDNET for highly ambiguous sublanguages such as the biomedical one.

2.2 Software Provided with WORDNET

To guarantee fast access to the entries and their relations, an optimized index file must be created. This is achieved through the easy-to-use GRIND software which comes with WORDNET. It simply consumes the lexicographic file(s) as input and creates two plain-text index files,[5] namely `data` and `index`. Furthermore, there is a command line tool, WN, and a graphical browser, WNB, for data visualization that require the specific index created by GRIND (as all the other tools that query the WORDNET data do as well). These tools are the most important (and only) means of software support for WORDNET creation by checking the syntax as well as allowing the (manual) inspection of the newly created index.

[5]Its syntax is described in http://wordnet.princeton.edu/man/wndb.5WN.

2.3 Third-Party WORDNET Tools

Due to the tremendous value of WORDNET for the NLP and IR community and its usefulness as a resource for coping with problems requiring massive amounts of lexico-semantic knowledge, the software-developing community was and continues to be quite active. Hence, in support of WORDNET several APIs and software tools were released that allow accessing, browsing and visualizing WORDNET data and measuring semantic similarity on the base of the WORDNET's lexical data structures.[6]

The majority of these APIs are maintained well and kept up to date, such as JAWS[7] and JWNL,[8] and enable connecting to the most recent version of WORDNET. For the calculation of various similarity measures, the PERL library WORDNET::SIMILARITY initiated and maintained by Ted Pedersen[9] can be considered as a *de facto* standard and has been used in various experimental settings and applications. This availability of well-documented and well-maintained software is definitely a strong argument to rely on WORDNET as a powerful lexico-semantic knowledge resource.

3 The BIOWORDNET Initiative

In this section, we describe our approach to extend WORDNET towards the biomedical domain by incorporating terminological resources from the OBO collection. The most obvious problems we faced were to define a common data format and to map non-compliant data formats to the chosen one.

3.1 OBO Ontologies

OBO is a collection of publicly accessible biomedical ontologies.[10] They cover terms from many biomedical subdomains and offer structured, domain-specific knowledge in terms of classes (which often come with synonyms and textual definitions) and class hierarchies. Besides the hierarchy-defining relation *is-a*, some OBO ontologies provide

[6]For a comprehensive overview of available WORDNET tools we refer to WORDNET's 'related project' website (http://wordnet.princeton.edu/links).

[7]http://engr.smu.edu/~tspell/

[8]http://jwordnet.sourceforge.net/

[9]http://wn-similarity.sourceforge.net/

[10]http://www.bioontology.org/

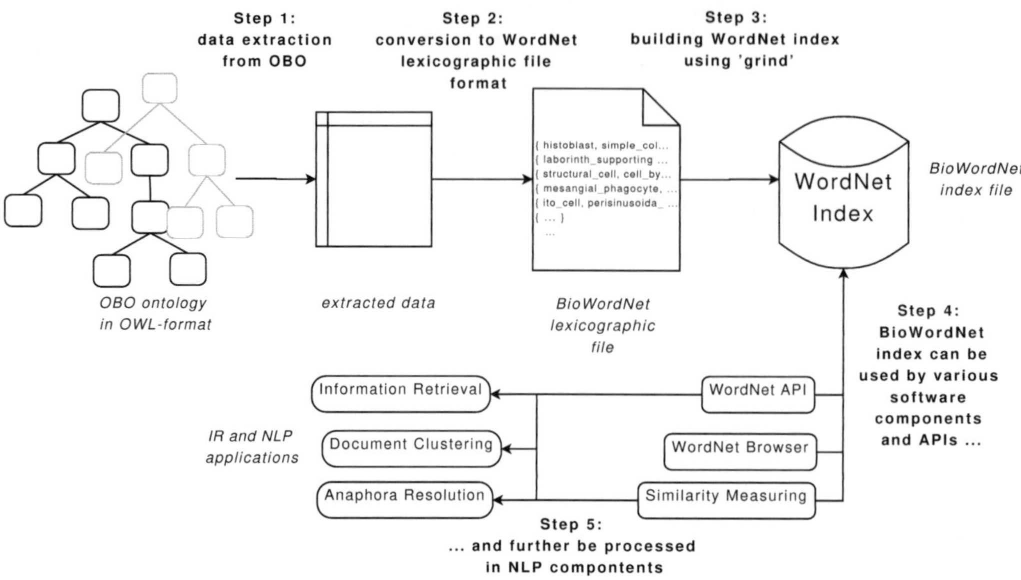

Figure 1: From OBO ontologies to BIOWORDNET— towards a domain-specific WORDNET for biomedicine

additional semantic relation types such as *sequence-of* or *develops-from* to express even more complex and finer-grained domain-specific knowledge. The ontologies vary significantly in size (up to 60,000 classes with more than 150,000 synonyms), the number of synonyms per term and the nature of terms.

The OBO ontologies are available in various formats including the OBO flat file format, XML and OWL. We chose to work with the OWL version for our purpose,[11] since for the OWL language also appropriate tools are available facilitating the extraction of particular information from the ontologies, such as taxonomic links, labels, synonyms and textual definitions of classes.

3.2 From OBO to BIOWORDNET

Our plan was to construct a BIOWORDNET by converting, in the first step, the OBO ontologies into a WORDNET hierarchy of synsets, while keeping to the WORDNET lexicographic file format, and building a WORDNET index. As a preparatory step, we defined a mapping from the ontology to WORDNET items as shown in Table 1.

The three-stage conversion approach is depicted in Figure 1. First, domain specific terms and taxonomic links between terms were extracted separately from each of the OBO ontologies. Then the extracted data was converted according to the syntax specifications of WORDNET's lexicographic file. Finally for each of the converted ontologies the WORDNET-specific index was built using GRIND.

OBO ontology	BIOWORDNET
ontology class	synset
class definition	synset gloss
class name	word in synset
synonym of class name	word in synset
C_i *is-a* C_j C_j *has-subclass* C_i	S_i *hyponym* of S_j S_j *hypernym* of S_i

Table 1: Mapping between items from OBO and from BIOWORDNET (C_i and C_j denote ontology classes, S_i and S_j the corresponding BIOWORDNET synsets)

Following this approach we ran into several problems, both regarding the WORDNET data structure and the WORDNET-related software that we used for the construction of the BIOWORDNET. Converting the OBO ontologies turned out to be cumbersome, especially the conversion of the CHEBI ontology[12] (long class names holding many special characters) and the NCI thesaurus[13] (large number

[11] http://www.w3.org/TR/owl-semantics/

[12] http://www.ebi.ac.uk/chebi/

[13] http://nciterms.nci.nih.gov/

of classes and some classes that also have a large number of subclasses). These and additional problems will be addressed in more detail in Section 4.

4 Problems with WORDNET's Data Format and Software Infrastructure

We here discuss two types of problems we found for the data format underlying the WORDNET lexicon and the software that helps building a WORDNET file and creating an index for this file. First, WORDNET's data structure puts several restrictions on what can be expressed in a WORDNET lexicon. For example, it constrains lexical information to a fixed number of homonyms and a fixed set of relations. Second, the data structure imposes a number of restrictions on the string format level. If these restrictions are violated the WORDNET processing software throws error messages which differ considerably in terms of informativeness for error tracing and detection or even do not surface at all at the lexicon builder's administration level.

4.1 Limitations of Expressiveness

The syntax on which the current WORDNET lexicographic file is based imposes severe limitations on what can be expressed in WORDNET. Although these limitations might be irrelevant for representing general-language terms, they do affect the construction of a WORDNET-like resource for biomedicine. To give some examples, the WORDNET format allows a 16-fold lexical ambiguity only (lexical IDs that are assigned to ambiguous words are restricted to the numbers 0-15, see Section 2). This forced us to neglect some of the OBO ontology class names and synonyms that were highly ambiguous.[14]

Furthermore, the OBO ontologies excel in a richer set of semantic relations than WORDNET can offer. Thus, a general problem with the conversion of the OBO ontologies into WORDNET format was that except from the taxonomic *is-a* relation (which corresponds to the WORDNET *hyponym* relation) and the *part-of* relation (which corresponds to the WORDNET *meronym* relation) all remaining OBO-specific relations (such as *develops-from*, *sequence-of*, *variant-of* and *position-of*) could not be represented in the BIOWORDNET. The structure of WORDNET neither contains such relations nor is it flexible enough to include them so that we face a systematic loss of information in BIOWORDNET compared to the original OBO ontologies. Although these restrictions are well-known, their removal would require extending the current WORDNET data structure fundamentally. This, in turn, would probably necessitate a full re-programming of all of WORDNET-related software.

[14]This is a well-known limitation that is already mentioned in the WORDNET documentation.

4.2 Limitations of Data Format and Software

When we tried to convert data extracted from the OBO ontologies into WORDNET's lexicographic file format (preserving its syntactic idiosyncrasies for the sake of quick and straightforward reusability of software add-ons), we encountered several intricacies that took a lot of time prior to building a valid lexicographic file.

First, we had to replace 31 different characters with unique strings such as "(" with "-LRB-" and "+" with "-PLU-" before GRIND was able to process the lexicographic file. The reason is that many of such special characters occurring in domain specific terms, especially in designators of chemical compounds such as *"methyl ester 2,10-dichloro-12H-dibenzo(d,g)(1,3)dioxocin-6-carboxylic acid"* (also known as *"treloxinate"* with the CAS registry number 30910-27-1), are reserved symbols in the WORDNET data formatting syntax. If these characters are not properly replaced GRIND throws an exact and useful error message (see Table 2, first row).

Second, we had to find out that we have to replace all empty glosses by at least one whitespace character. Otherwise, GRIND informs the user in terms of a rather cryptic error message that mentions the position of the error though not its reason (see Table 2, second row).

Third, numbers at the end of a lexical item need to be escaped. In WORDNET, the string representation of an item is used as its unique identifier. To distinguish homonyms (words with the same spelling but different meaning, such as *"cell"* as the functional unit of all organisms, on the one hand, and as small compartment, on the other hand) according to the WORDNET format different numbers from 0 to 15 (so-called lexical IDs) have to be appended

Problem Description	Sample Error Message	Usefulness of Error Message	Problem Solution
illegal use of key characters	*noun.cell, line 7: Illegal character %*	high	replace illegal characters
empty gloss	*sanity error - actual pos 2145 != assigned pos 2143!*	moderate	add gloss consisting of at least one whitespace character
homonyms (different words with identical strings)	*noun.rex, line 5: Synonym "electrochemical_reaction" is not unique in file*	high	distinguish word senses by adding lexical identifiers (use the numbers 1-15)
lexical ID larger than 15	*noun.rex, line 4: ID must be less than 16: cd25*	high	quote trailing numbers of words, only assign lexical identifiers between 1-15, omit additional word senses
word with more than 425 characters	*Segmentation fault (core dumped)*	low	omit words that exceed the maximal length of 425 characters
synset with more than 998 direct hyponymous synsets	*Segmentation fault (core dumped)*	low	omit some hyponymous synsets or introduce intermediate synsets with a limited number of hyponymous synsets
no query result though the synset is in the index, access software crashes	none	–	not known

Table 2: Overview of the different kinds of problems that we encountered when creating a BIOWORDNET keeping to the WORDNET data structure and the corresponding software. Each problem description is followed by a sample error message that GRIND had thrown, a statement about how useful the error message was to detect the source of the error and a possible solution for the problems, if available. The last row documents a special experience with data viewers for data from the NCI thesaurus.

to the end of each homonym. If in a lexicographic file two identical strings occur that have not been assigned different lexical identifiers (it does not matter whether this happens within or across synsets) GRIND emits an error message that mentions both, the position and the lexical entry which caused this error (cf. Table 2, third row).

Numbers that appear at the end of a lexical item as an integral part of it (such as *"2"* in *"IL2"*, a special type of cytokine (protein)) have to be escaped in order to avoid their misinterpretation as lexical identifiers. This, again, is a well-documented shortcoming of WORDNET's data specification rules.

In case such numbers are not escaped prior to presenting the lexicographic file to GRIND the word closing numbers are always interpreted as lexical identifiers. Closing numbers that exceed the number 15 cause GRIND to throw an informative error message (see Table 2, fourth row).

4.3 Undocumented Restrictions and Insufficient Error Messages

In addition to the more or less documented restrictions of the WORDNET data format mentioned above we found additional restrictions that lack documentation up until now, to the best of our knowledge.

First, it seems that the length of a word is restricted to 425 characters. If a word in the lexicographic file exceeds this length, GRIND is not able to create an index and throws an empty error message, namely the memory error "segmentation fault" (cf. Table 2, fifth row). As a consequence of this restriction, some very long CHEBI class names could not have been included in the BIOWORDNET.

Second, it seems that synsets are only allowed to group up to 988 direct hyponymous synsets. Again, GRIND is not able to create an index, if this restriction is not obeyed and throws the null memory error message "segmentation fault" (cf. Table 2, sixth row). An NCI thesaurus class that had more than 998 direct subclasses thus could not have been included in the BIOWORDNET.

Due to insufficient documentation and utterly general error messages the only way to locate the problem causing the "segmentation fault" errors was to examine the lexicographic files manually. We had to reduce the number of synset entries in the lexicographic file, step by step, in a kind of trial and error approach until we could resolve the problem. This is, no doubt, a highly inefficient and time consuming procedure. More informative error messages of GRIND would have helped us a lot.

4.4 Deceptive Results from WORDNET Software and Third-Party Components

After getting rid of all previously mentioned errors, valid index files were compiled. It was possible to access these index files using the WORDNET querying tools WN and WNB, indicating the index files were 'valid'. However, when we tried to query the index file that was generated by GRIND for the NCI thesaurus we got strange results. While WN did not return any query results, the browser WNB crashed without any error message (cf. Table 2, seventh row). The same holds for the Java APIs JAWS and JWNL.

Since a manual examination of the index file revealed that the entries that we were searching for, in fact, were included in the file, some other, up to this step unknown error must have prevented the software tools from finding the targeted entries. Hence, we want to point out that although we have examined this error for the NCI thesaurus only, the risk is high that this "no show" error is likely to bias any other application as well which makes use of the the same software that we grounded our experiments on. Since the NCI thesaurus is a very large resource, even worse, further manual error search is nearly impossible. At this point, we stopped our attempt building a WORDNET resource for biomedicine based on the WORDNET formatting and software framework.

5 Related Work

In the literature dealing with WORDNET and its structures from a resource perspective (rather than dealing with its applications), two directions can be distinguished. On the one hand, besides the original English WORDNET and the various variant WORDNETs for other languages (Vossen, 1998), extensions to particular domains have already been proposed (for the medical domain by Buitelaar and Sacaleanu (2002) and Fellbaum et al. (2006); for the architectural domain Bentivogli et al. (2004); and for the technical report domain by Vossen (2001)). However, none of these authors neither mentions implementation details of the WORDNETs or performance pitfalls we have encountered, nor is supplementary software pointed out that might be useful for our work.

On the other hand, there are suggestions concerning novel representation formats of next-generation WORDNETs. For instance in the BALKANET project (Tufiş et al., 2004), an XML schema plus a DTD was proposed (Smrž, 2004) and an editor called CISDIC with basic maintenance functionalities and consistency check was released (Horák and Smrž, 2004). The availability of APIs or software to measure similarity though remains an open issue.

So, our approach to reuse the structure and the software for building a BIOWORDNET was motivated by the fact that we could not find any alternatives coming with a software ensemble as described in Section 2. Against all expectations, we did not manage to reuse the WORDNET data structure. However, there are no publications that report on such difficulties and pitfalls we were confronted with.

6 Discussion and Conclusion

We learnt from our conversion attempt that the current WORDNET representation format of WORDNET suffers from several limitations and idiosyncrasies that cannot be by-passed by a simple, yet ad hoc work-around. Many of the limitations and pitfalls we found limiting (in the sense what can be expressed in WORDNET) are due to the fact that its data format is out-of-date and not really suitable for the biomedical sublanguage. In addition, though we do not take into doubt that the WORDNET software works fine for the official WORDNET release, our experiences taught us that it fails or gives limited support in case of building and debugging a new WORDNET resource. Even worse, we have evidence from one large terminological resource (NCI) that WORDNET's software infrastructure (GRIND) renders deceptive results.

Although WORDNET might no longerbe the one and only lexical resource for NLP each year a continuously strong stream of publications on the use of WORDNET illustrates its importance for the community. On this account we find it remarkable that although improvements in content and structure of WORDNET have been proposed (e.g., Boyd-Graber et al. (2006) propose to add (weighted) connections between synsets, Oltramari et al. (2002) suggest to restructure WORDNET's taxonomical structure, and Mihalcea and Moldovan (2001) recommend to merge synsets that are too fine-grained) to the best of our knowledge, no explicit proposals have been made to improve the representation format of WORDNET in combination with the adaption of the WORDNET-related software.

According to our experiences the existing WORDNET software is hardly (re)usable due to insufficient error messages that the software throws and limited documentation. From our point of view it would be highly preferable if the software would be improved and made more user-supportive (more meaningful error messages would already improve the usefulness of the software). In terms of the actual representation format of WORDNET we found that using the current format is not only cumbersome and error-prone, but also limits what can be expressed in a WORDNET resource.

From our perspective this indicates the need for a major redesign of WORDNET's data structure foundations to keep up with the standards of today's meta data specification languages (e.g., based on RFD (Graves and Gutierrez, 2006), XML or OWL (Lüngen et al., 2007)). We encourage the re-implementation of WORDNET resources based on such a state-of-the-art markup language (for OWL in particular a representation of WORDNET is already available, cf. van Assem et al. (2006)). Of course, if a new representation format is used for a WORDNET resource also the software accessing the resource has to be adapted to the new format. This may require substantial implementation efforts that we think are worth to be spent, if the new format overcomes the major problems that are due to the original WORDNET format.

Acknowledgments

This work was funded by the German Ministry of Education and Research within the STEMNET project (01DS001A-C) and by the EC within the BOOTSTREP project (FP6-028099).

References

Luisa Bentivogli, Andrea Bocco, and Emanuele Pianta. 2004. ARCHIWORDNET: Integrating WORDNET with domain-specific knowledge. In Petr Sojka, Karel Pala, Christiane Fellbaum, and Piek Vossen, editors, *GWC 2004 – Proceedings of the 2nd International Conference of the Global WordNet Association*, pages 39–46. Brno, Czech Republic, January 20-23, 2004.

Olivier Bodenreider and Anita Burgun. 2002. Characterizing the definitions of anatomical concepts in WORDNET and specialized sources. In *Proceedings of the 1st International Conference of the Global WordNet Association*, pages 223–230. Mysore, India, January 21-25, 2002.

Jordan Boyd-Graber, Christiane Fellbaum, Daniel Osherson, and Robert Schapire. 2006. Adding dense, weighted connections to WORDNET. In Petr Sojka, Key-Sun Choi, Christiane Fellbaum, and Piek Vossen, editors, *GWC 2006 – Proceedings of the 3rd International* WORDNET *Conference*, pages 29–35. South Jeju Island, Korea, January 22-26, 2006.

Paul Buitelaar and Bogdan Sacaleanu. 2002. Extending synsets with medical terms WORDNET and specialized sources. In *Proceedings of the 1st International Conference of the Global WordNet Association*. Mysore, India, January 21-25, 2002.

Anita Burgun and Olivier Bodenreider. 2001. Comparing terms, concepts and semantic classes in WORDNET and the UNIFIED MEDICAL LANGUAGE SYSTEM. In *Proceedings of the NAACL 2001 Workshop 'WORDNET and Other Lexical Resources: Applications, Extensions and Customizations'*, pages 77–82. Pittsburgh, PA, June 3-4, 2001. New Brunswick, NJ: Association for Computational Linguistics.

José Castaño, Jason Zhang, and James Pustejovsky. 2002. Anaphora resolution in biomedical literature. In *Proceedings of The International Symposium on Reference Resolution for Natural Language Processing*. Alicante, Spain, June 3-4, 2002.

Christiane Fellbaum, Udo Hahn, and Barry Smith. 2006. Towards new information resources for public health:

From WORDNET to MEDICAL WORDNET. *Journal of Biomedical Informatics*, 39(3):321–332.

Christiane Fellbaum, editor. 1998. WORDNET*: An Electronic Lexical Database*. Cambridge, MA: MIT Press.

Alvaro Graves and Caludio Gutierrez. 2006. Data representations for WORDNET: A case for RDF. In Petr Sojka, Key-Sun Choi, Christiane Fellbaum, and Piek Vossen, editors, *GWC 2006 – Proceedings of the 3rd International* WORDNET *Conference*, pages 165–169. South Jeju Island, Korea, January 22-26, 2006.

Udo Hahn, Martin Romacker, and Stefan Schulz. 1999. Discourse structures in medical reports – watch out! The generation of referentially coherent and valid text knowledge bases in the MEDSYNDIKATE system. *International Journal of Medical Informatics*, 53(1):1–28.

Sanda M. Harabagiu, Răzvan C. Bunescu, and Steven J. Maiorano. 2001. Text and knowledge mining for coreference resolution. In *NAACL'01, Language Technologies 2001 – Proceedings of the 2nd Meeting of the North American Chapter of the Association for Computational Linguistics*, pages 1–8. Pittsburgh, PA, USA, June 2-7, 2001. San Francisco, CA: Morgan Kaufmann.

Deirdre Hogan. 2007. Coordinate noun phrase disambiguation in a generative parsing model. In *ACL'07 – Proceedings of the 45th Annual Meeting of the Association of Computational Linguistics*, pages 680–687. Prague, Czech Republic, June 28-29, 2007. Stroudsburg, PA: Association for Computational Linguistics.

Aleş Horák and Pavel Smrž. 2004. New features of wordnet editor VisDic. *Romanian Journal of Information Science and Technology (Special Issue)*, 7(1-2):201–213.

Harald Lüngen, Claudia Kunze, Lothar Lemnitzer, and Angelika Storrer. 2007. Towards an integrated OWL model for domain-specific and general language WordNets. In Attila Tanács, Dorá Csendes, Veronika Vincze, Christiane Fellbaum, and Piek Vossen, editors, *GWC 2008 – Proceedings of the 4th Global* WORDNET *Conference*, pages 281–296. Szeged, Hungary, January 22-25, 2008.

Rada Mihalcea and Dan Moldovan. 2001. EZ.WORDNET: Principles for automatic generation of a coarse grained WORDNET. In *Proceedings of the 14th International Florida Artificial Intelligence Research Society (FLAIRS) Conference*, pages 454–458.

Alessandro Oltramari, Aldo Gangemi, Nicola Guarino, and Claudio Madolo. 2002. Restructuring WORDNET's top-level. In *Proceedings of ONTOLEX 2002 @ LREC 2002*.

Siddharth Patwardhan, Satanjeev Banerjee, and Ted Pedersen. 2003. Using measures of semantic relatedness for word sense disambiguation. In Alexander F. Gelbukh, editor, *CICLing 2003 – Computational Linguistics and Intelligent Text Processing. Proceedings of the 4th International Conference*, volume 2588 of *Lecture Notes in Computer Science*, pages 241–257. Mexico City, Mexico, February 16-22, 2003. Berlin etc.: Springer.

Ted Pedersen, Siddharth Patwardhan, and Jason Michelizzi. 2004. WORDNET::Similarity: Measuring the relatedness of concepts. In *AAAI'04 – Proceedings of the 19th National Conference on Artificial Intelligence & IAAI'04 – Proceedings of the 16th Innovative Applications of Artificial Intelligence Conference*, pages 1024–1025. San José, CA, USA, July 25-29, 2004. Menlo Park, CA; Cambridge, MA: AAAI Press & MIT Press.

Michael Poprat and Udo Hahn. 2007. Quantitative data on referring expressions in biomedical abstracts. In *BioNLP at ACL 2007 – Proceedings of the Workshop on Biological, Translational, and Clinical Language Processing*, pages 193–194. Prague, Czech Republic, June 29, 2007. Stroudsburg, PA: Association for Computational Liguistics.

Pavel Smrž. 2004. Quality control and checking for wordnets development: A case study of BALKANET. *Romanian Journal of Information Science and Technology (Special Issue)*, 7(1-2):173–181.

D. Tufiş, D. Christea, and S. Stamou. 2004. BALKANET: Aims, methods, results and perspectives. a general overview. *Romanian Journal of Information Science and Technology (Special Issue)*, 7(1-2):9–43.

Mark van Assem, Aldo Gangemi, and Guus Schreiber. 2006. Conversion of WORDNET to a standard RDF/OWL representation. In *LREC 2006 – Proceedings of the 5th International Conference on Language Resources and Evaluation*. Genoa, Italy, May 22-28, 2006. Paris: European Language Resources Association (ELRA), available on CD.

Piek Vossen, editor. 1998. EUROWORDNET*: A Multilingual Database with Lexical Semantic Networks*. Dordrecht: Kluwer Academic Publishers.

Piek Vossen. 2001. Extending, trimming and fusing WORDNET for technical documents. In *Proceedings of the NAACL 2001 Workshop* 'WORDNET *and Other Lexical Resources: Applications, Extensions and Customizations'*. Pittsburgh, PA, June 3-4, 2001. New Brunswick, NJ: Association for Computational Linguistics.

Fast, Scalable and Reliable Generation of Controlled Natural Language

David Hardcastle
Faculty of Maths, Computing and Technology
The Open University
Milton Keynes, UK
d.w.hardcastle@open.ac.uk

Richard Power
Faculty of Maths, Computing and Technology
The Open University
Milton Keynes, UK
r.power@open.ac.uk

Abstract

In this paper we describe a natural language generation system which takes as its input a set of assertions encoded as a semantic graph and outputs a data structure connecting the semantic graph to a text which expresses those assertions, encoded as a TAG syntactic tree. The scope of the system is restricted to controlled natural language, and this allows the generator to work within a tightly restricted domain of locality. We can exploit this feature of the system to ensure fast and efficient generation, and also to make the generator reliable by providing a rapid algorithm which can exhaustively test at compile time the completeness of the linguistic resources with respect to the range of potential meanings. The system can be exported for deployment with a minimal build of the semantic and linguistic resources that is verified to ensure that no runtime errors will result from missing resources. The framework is targeted at using natural language generation technology to build semantic web applications where machine-readable information can be automatically expressed in natural language on demand.

1 Introduction

This paper describes a fast, reliable and scalable framework for developing applications supporting tactical generation – by which we mean applications which take as their input some semantic structure that has already been organised at a high level, and choose the syntactic structures and words required to express it. The framework takes as input a semantic graph representing a set of assertions in Description Logic (DL) (Baader et al., 2003) and transforms it into a tree which encodes the grammar rules, syntactic subcategorisations, orderings and lexical anchors required to construct a textual representation of the input data. The resulting text is *conceptually aligned*, by which we mean that each component of the text structure (such as words, clauses or sentences, for example) is linked back to the mediating structure from which the text was generated, and from there back to vertices and edges in the semantic graph received as input. The target context for the framework is the construction of semantic web (Berners-Lee et al., 2001) resources using Natural Language Generation (NLG) technology which extends the notion of semantic alignment developed in the WYSIWYM system (Power and Scott, 1998; Power et al., 2003). In this context the text is ephemeral and is generated on demand, while the document content is fully machine-readable, supporting tasks such as automated consistency checking, inferencing and semantic search/query. Since the text is fully linked to the underlying semantic representation it supports a rich user interface encompassing fast and reliable semantic search, inline syntax or anaphora highlighting, knowledge editing, and so on. Finally, the text could be generated in many different natural languages making the information content more widely available. We envisage the technology supporting a range of different use cases such as information feeds, technical instructions, medical orders or short, factual reports.

For such a system to be of practical value in an enterprise system the NLG component must sup-

Software Engineering, Testing, and Quality Assurance for Natural Language Processing, pages 40–48,
Columbus, Ohio, USA, June 2008. ©2008 Association for Computational Linguistics

port standard aspects of software engineering quality such as modularity, reliability, speed and scalability. The design of the framework relies on two key simplifying assumptions and these limit the range of information which can be represented and the fluency of the text used to express it. Specifically, the information is limited by the expressivity of DL – for example only limited quantification is possible – and the surface text is restricted to controlled natural language (Hartley and Paris, 2001). The upside of this trade-off is that the domain of locality is very restricted. This means that there is minimal search during generation and so the algorithm is fast and scalable. It also enables us to design the generator so that it is predictable and can therefore be statically tested for *completeness*, a notion which we define in Section 3.

Our aim in this paper is to show how the simplifying assumptions behind the design bring considerable engineering benefits. We discuss the theoretical background to our approach (Sections 2 and 3) and then present the implementation details, focusing on the features of the design that support speed and scalability (Section 4) and reliability (Section 5), followed by an overview of the architectural considerations (Section 6). Finally we present the results of tests evaluating the system's performance (Section 7).

2 Implementation Theory

The generation algorithm has its roots in the WYSIWYM system, which was originally developed as a way of defining the input for multilingual NLG in DRAFTER (Paris et al., 1995), one of a series of projects in the KPML/Penman tradition (Bateman et al., 1989). The system uses the standard semantic representation employed in DL and the Semantic Web: a Terminology Box, or *Tbox*, defining the concepts and their interrelations and an Assertion Box, or *Abox*, representing the information content that forms the input (Baader et al., 2003). An Abox is a set of assertions defining relations between instances of the types defined in the Tbox. It can be depicted by a connected graph (Figure 1) in which vertices represent entities and edges represent relations, and is represented in the input to the system by a set of RDF subject-predicate-argument triples (Lassila

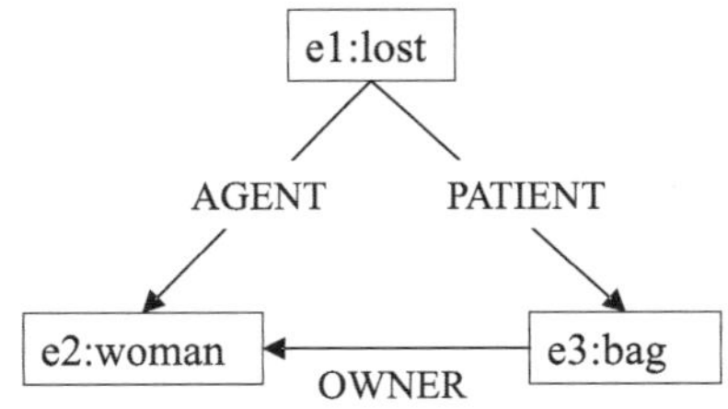

Figure 1: Sample Abox

and Swick, 1998), with one-place predications assigning types and two-place predications asserting relationships. Assuming that the entities are being mentioned for the first time, we might express this Abox fragment in English by the sentence 'a woman lost her bag'[1]. This sentence can be aligned with the Abox by associating spans of the text with the entities expressed by the Abox, as follows:

Span	**Entity**	**Context**
a woman lost her bag	e_1	ROOT
a woman	e_2	AGENT
her bag	e_3	PATIENT
her	e_2	OWNER

Note that the same entity may be expressed in multiple contexts (denoted by the incoming arcs in the semantic graph). The relationships between the entities are represented by syntactic dependencies between the spans of the text. For instance, AGENT(e_1,e_2) is realised by the clause-subject relation between 'a woman lost her bag' and its subspan 'a woman'. This direct linking of semantic and syntactic dependencies has of course been noted many times, for instance in Meaning-Text Theory (Candito and Kahane, 1998).

The structure of the spans of text can be represented by a reconfiguration of the original Abox as an ordered tree, which we will henceforth call an *Atree*. Figure 2 shows an Atree that fits the example Abox. Note that since this is a tree, the vertex with two incoming edges (e_2) has to be repeated, and there are two spans referring to the woman.

[1] The system is able to generate a referring expression, 'her', for the second reference to the woman since it knows that the entity has already been mentioned in the text. This information is available because the Atree, see Figure 2, is an ordered structure.

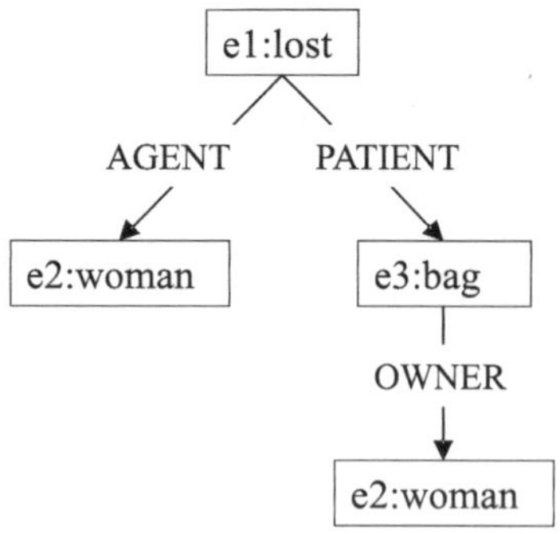

Figure 2: Sample Atree

This Atree is constructed using a set of bindings which map instances of concepts from the Tbox in a given context onto a subcategorisation frame, grammar rule call and list of lexical anchors. As each vertex of the Atree is constructed it is labelled with the grammar rule and lexical anchors and linked back to the vertex of the Abox which it expresses. Our current model uses the Tree Adjoining Grammar (TAG) formalism, see Joshi (1987), and the Atree acts as a stand-in *derivation tree* from which the derived syntactic tree can be computed. Each vertex of the derived tree is linked back to the vertex of the Atree from which it was generated, and so the output from the system is a composite data structure comprising the Tbox, Abox, Atree and derived tree with a chain of references connecting each span of the surface text via the Atree to the underlying semantic representation. A detailed exposition of the process through which the Atree and derivation tree are constructed is presented in a separate Technical Report (Hardcastle and Power, 2008).

2.1 Simplifying assumptions

The design of the generator relies on two simplifying assumptions. The key assumption for this paper is that the text should adhere strictly to a controlled language, so that a given local semantic configuration is always realised by the same linguistic pattern. The cost is that the text is likely to be repetitive and may be awkward at times; however the trade-off is that the domain of locality is tightly restricted and this yields important benefits in speed, scalability, reliability and verifiability that make the system suitable for deployment in an enterprise environment.

We also assume that the strategic element of the NLG process, comprising content selection and document structuring, has occurred prior to our system receiving its input. Our framework is focused specifically on tactical generation – rendering the semantic representation of the selected content as text.

3 Completeness

We can verify that the generator is *complete*, in the sense that we can guarantee that it will produce a derivation tree for any Abox valid under the Tbox. We present the details of the verification algorithm below, in Section 5. Note that we assume that the system is equipped with the requisite morphological and orthographic rules to realise the resulting derivation tree. We also note that we cannot verify that the generator is *consistent*, by which we mean that it should produce different texts for different Aboxes, nor that the syntactic frames and lexical anchors mapped to the concepts in the Tbox are appropriate. Checking the system for consistency remains an open research question.

4 Speed and Scalability

In many NLG systems the choice of syntactic structure and lexical arguments depends on a large number of interdependent variables. This means that the process of realizing the semantic input involves exploring a large search space, often with some backtracking. In contrast, the algorithm described in this paper is monotonic and involves minimal search. The system begins at the root of the Abox and uses a set of mappings to construct the Atree one node at a time. Because the same local semantic context is always expressed in the same way the choice of syntactic structure and lexical arguments can always be made on the basis of a single mapping. Over the course of this section we demonstrate this with a simple example using resources that were automatically inferred to construct the test harness described in Section 8, which could be used to construct the following simple sentence:

> The nurse reminded the doctor that the patient was allergic to aspirin.

The Abox representing this sentence is rooted in an instance of a Tbox concept representing an event in which one person reminds another of a fact. Figure 3 shows the attributes defined for this Tbox concept, *938B*, namely an *actor*, *actee* and *target*. The range of *actor* and *actee* is any concept in the Tbox subsumed by the *person* concept, the range of *target* is any *fact*. There will therefore be three out-going arcs from the root Abox node, labelled with attributes *actor*, *actee* and *target*, pointing respectively to nodes representing the nurse, doctor and the fact about the patient's allergy described in the sample sentence above. Some of these nodes will themselves have out-going arcs expressing their own attributes, such as the subsidiary details of the fact about the allergy.

```
938B
    actor(person)
    actee(person)
    target(fact)
```

Figure 3: A Sample Tbox Node

To realize the first node in the Abox the system searches for mappings for concept *938B*. The controlled language assumption allows the system to search with a restricted domain of locality, and so the only variables affecting the choice of frame will be: the Tbox concept represented by the Abox node to be realized (*938B* in this case), the syntactic context (there is none at this stage since we are processing the root node, so the system will default to *clause* context), the incoming arc (there is none at this stage so no constraint is applied), the out-going arcs (the three attributes specified), and whether or not the instance has already been expressed (in this case it has not)[2]. The search parameters are used to locate a mapping such as the one depicted in Figure 4 below.

```
<frame concept="938B"
      role="any"
      subcat="CatClause-33"
      bindings="SUB,D_OB,CL_COM">
   <gr key="TnxOVnx1s2">
      <anchor lemma="remind" pos="verb"/>
   </gr>
</frame>
```

Figure 4: A Sample Mapping

This mapping tells the system which subcategorisation frame to use, which grammar rule to associate with it, which lexical anchors to pass as arguments to the grammar rule and also how to order the subsidiary arguments of the subcategorisation frame (the *bindings* attribute in the *frame* element). The subcategorisation frame itself (shown in Figure 5) is highly reusable as it only defines a coarse-grained syntactic type and a list of arguments, each of which consists of a free text label (such as *SUB* indicating the subject syntactic dependency) and a coarse-grained syntactic constraint such as *clause*, *nominal* or *modifier*. In this example the first attribute of the *938B* node, namely the *actor*, is mapped to the *SUB* (subject) argument, so it will become the first child of the Atree node representing the *remind* event. The *nominal* syntactic constraint will be carried forward as the syntactic context for the *nurse* node of the Abox, constraining the choice of mapping that the system can make to realise it. So, each mapping enforces an ordering on the out-going arcs of the Abox which is used to order the Atree and provides a syntactic context which is used to constrain

```
CatClause-33
   type= CLAUSE
   args= SUB/NOMINAL,
         D_OB/NOMINAL,
         CL_COM/CLAUSE
```

Figure 5: Sample Subcategorisation Frame

[2]The last of these variables is used to determine whether or not a referring expression (an anaphoric reference to an entity which has already been mentioned) is required. Because the Atree is ordered and is constructed in order, the system always knows whether an instance is being mentioned for the first time. We currently render subsequent mentions by pruning all of the out-going arcs from the Abox node, which also allows us to manage cycles in the semantic graph. Since the system knows which nodes in the semantic graph have already been mentioned it would also be possible to configure an external call to a GRE system (Dale, 1989) - an application which infers the content of a referring expression given the current semantic context.

the mapping search for each child. The process of locating and imposing mappings cascades through the Abox from the root with minimal search and no backtracking. If multiple mappings are defined for a given context the first one is always chosen. If no mapping is located then the system fails.

While the Atree is constructed, it is annotated with the grammar rules and lexical anchors listed in each mapping, allowing it to serve as a stand-in TAG derivation tree from which a derived syntactic tree can be constructed by instantiating and connecting the elementary trees specified by each grammar rule. Further details of this process are given in a Technical Report (Hardcastle and Power, 2008).

So while the controlled language assumption that we should always express the same local semantic context in the same way limits expressivity, it also limits algorithmic choice and prevents backtracking, which means that the system can generate rapidly and scale linearly. In the following section we show how we can prove at compile time that no Abox can be constructed which will result in a local semantic context not accounted for in the mappings.

5 Reliability

In a real-world context the Tbox will evolve as the underlying domain model is extended and enhanced. As a result, some of the mappings described above will become defunct and in some instances a required mapping will not be present. If the system encounters an Abox which requires a mapping that is not present it will not backtrack but will fail, making the system fragile. To address this problem we need to be able to run a static test in a short period of time to determine if any mappings are unused or missing.

Although the set of possible Abox graphs is an infinite set, the tight domain of locality means that there is a finite set of parameters which could be passed to the generator for any given Tbox. As described in the previous section the choice of mapping is based only on the following information: the concept being realised, the syntactic context, the number of attributes expressed by the concept, the attribute used to select it, and whether or not this Abox instance is being mentioned for the first time. Given a starting TBox node and syntactic context the system can crawl the TBox recursively using the subcategorisation frames returned from each parameter set to derive a new list of parameter sets to be tested. Each of these must be tested both as a first and as a subsequent mention. The result is an algorithm which proves the application's *completeness* (as defined in Section 3) with respect to a particular domain (represented by the Tbox); if the test succeeds then it guarantees that the mappings defined by the system can transform any Abox that is valid under the given domain into an Atree annotated with the information required to produce a derived syntactic tree.

As above, the proving algorithm starts with a root concept in the Tbox and an initial syntactic context and uses these as the starting parameter set to find the first mapping. Once a mapping is located it explores each of the attributes of the root concept using the syntactic context to which the attribute is bound by the mapping. Since there is no Abox it constructs a list of parameter sets to check using every concept in the range of the attribute.

For example, during the verification process the prover will encounter the mapping shown above in Figure 4 for the *remind* concept *938B* in a clausal context. The concept has three attributes: an *actor*, an *actee* and a *target*. The first of these has as its range all of the subconcepts of *person* defined in the Tbox, and this introduces a new sub-problem. The first attribute is bound to the *SUB* argument of the subcategorisation frame used in the mapping, in Figure 4, by the *bindings* element, and this argument of the subcategorisation frame imposes a nominal constraint. So the fact that concept *938B* might need to be expressed using this mapping means that any subconcept of *person* might need to be expressed in a nominal syntactic context with semantic role *actor*, and so the prover now checks each subconcept with these parameters. If none of the subconcepts of *person* define any attributes and a mapping is found for each then no new sub-problems are introduced and so this branch of the search bottoms out.

The prover then returns to *938B* and processes the *actee* and *target* attributes. The *target* attribute is bound to the *CL_COM* argument of the subcategorisation frame, and so the new sub-problem involves checking that every subconcept of *fact* can be expressed as a clause with semantic role *target*. In the ontology the subconcepts of *fact* include *events*, each of which define a number of attributes, and so this sub-problem branches out into many new sub-problems before it bottoms out. One such *event* will be the concept *938B*, but since the mapping that we have already encountered (Figure 4) is encoded for any semantic role and the system has already processed it the prover can break out and does not fall into an infinite loop. This checking process continues recursively until the search space is exhausted, with each parameter set tested being cached to reduce the size of the search space.

6 Relaxing the Simplifying Constraints

The simplifying assumptions described in Section 2.1 deliver benefits in terms of performance and reliability; however, they limit the expressivity of the language and reduce the scope of what can be expressed. We can relax some of the constraints imposed by the simplifying assumptions and still have a performant and reliable system, although proving completeness becomes more complex and some localised exponential complexity is introduced into the generation algorithm. In this section we explore the ways in which relaxing the constraints to allow quantification or underspecification impact on the system.

The simplest scenario, which adheres to our simplifying constraints, is that each node in the Abox expresses exactly one of each of the attributes defined by the Tbox concept which it instantiates. So, using the *remind* example above, every instance of *remind* must express an *actor*, an *actee* and a *fact*. In practice the Tbox may allow an attribute not to be expressed, to be expressed many times or to be expressed but not specified. We handle the first case by allowing arguments in the subcategorisation frames to be marked as optional; for example, a verb frame may include an optional *adverb* slot. These optional arguments increase the number of tests that must be performed; if a frame has n optional slots then the system will need to perform 2^n checks to verify it, and will have to consider 2^n mapping combinations during generation. This introduces localised exponentiation into both the generation and the verification algorithm, although it will only lead to tractability problems if the number of optional slots on any single frame is too high, since the exponent is *only* applied to each frame and not across the whole search space.

Where an attribute may remain unspecified the system can be configured to respond in two different ways. First, unspecified attributes can be included in the text using the concept that represents the root of the range. For example, if an event occurs at a time which is not specified then the system can use the concept that represents the root of the range (e.g. *timePeriod* perhaps) and render it accordingly ("at some time"). Alternatively the system can prune all underspecified instances from the Abox before the Atree is generated. Attributes which may not be expressed (for either reason) must be flagged in the TBox so that the proving algorithm knows to match them to optional arguments in the subcategorisation frames. This is implemented with a flag on each attribute definition indicating whether its presence in the Abox is optional.

Relaxing the constraints also impacts on our ability to verify the grammar rules which are associated with each mapping. If we use TAG, then we can easily verify that the syntactic type of the root of the elementary tree defined by each mapping matches the syntactic type of the subcategorisation frame to which it is bound. However, if a mapping can be accessed via an optional slot in another subcategorisation frame, then it must be bound to an *auxiliary* tree, that is to an elementary tree which can be added to the derived tree through adjunction, since any derived tree with open substitution sites will be grammatically incomplete. For the system to support this behaviour each mapping must declare not just the concept which it realises but also the role (Tbox attribute) which it fulfils, so that both the prover can determine whether it may be left out, and this increases the combinatorial complexity of the algorithm.

7 Architecture

The design of the generator ensures that it can generate rapidly and that it can be verified at compile time. A further feature is that it is implemented with a component-based modular architecture. For NLP applications it is particularly important that individual components can be independently verified and reused, because linguistic resources are time-consuming and expensive to build and curate. Furthermore, because the mappings from concepts to subcategorisation frames, grammar rules and lexical anchors are defined in a single file, the task of building and maintaining the mappings is easier to learn and easier to manage. It is also easier to bootstrap the mappings through resource mining, as we did ourselves in the construction of the test data set discussed in Section 8.

The framework manages the graph and tree structures and the transformations between them, and it defines the API for the domain and language specific resources that will be required by the application. It also defines the API of the linguistic resource manager, leaving it to the application layer to provide an appropriate implementer using dependency injection (Fowler, 2004). Rather than define a core 'interlingual' feature structure that attempts to capture all of the lexical features used by the grammar, the framework provides a genericised interface to the linguistic resource manager. This means that grammars for different natural languages can use different feature structures to define the lexical anchors used by the application and to support tasks that are the responsibility of the grammar, such as unification or morphological inflection. For example, all verbs in French should have a flag indicating whether *avoir* or *être* is used as a modal auxiliary for the *passé composé*, but this flag need not be present for other languages. The Tbox, the subcategorisation frames and the mappings between them are all defined as data sources and can be reused across applications as appropriate. Although they are not defined in code they can still be verified at compile time by the prover discussed in the previous section, and this allows the system to be flexible and modular without introducing the risk of runtime failures caused by faulty mapping data.

7.1 Export

A further feature of the system which arises from the proving algorithm is that it supports export behaviour. In an enterprise context we want to be able to reuse linguistic resource components, such as a lexicon, a grammar, a morphological generator and so on, across many different applications. These resources are large and complex and for a given application much of the data may not be required. Because the proving algorithm is able to compile a comprehensive list of the concepts, grammatical relations, subcategorisation frames and lexical anchors that will be required to realise any Abox, given a starting concept and syntactic context, the system can cut the Tbox, lexicon, grammar, subcategorisation frame store and related resources to export a build for deployment, while guaranteeing that the deployed application will never fail because of a missing resource. This is of particular value if we want to reuse large-scale, generic, curated resources for a small domain and deploy where bandwidth is an issue – for example where language generation is required in a client-heavy internet-based or mobile application.

8 Testing and Results

We unit-tested the mechanics of the framework, such as the graph and tree managers. We then built a proof-of-concept application with a small ontology representing the domain of patient treatment narratives and handcrafted the subcategorisation frames, lexical resources and TAG grammars for English, French, Spanish and Italian. We used this application to verify the independence of the framework, domain and linguistic resources and verified that we could develop linguistic resources offline and plug them into the application effectively. The application also served as a test harness to test the adaptibility of the framework to render the same semantic context in different syntactic structures depending on the target natural language. For example, we included the examination of a body part belonging to a person in the domain, and this was expressed through a Saxon genitive in English but a prepositional phrase (with the subsidiary NPs in the reverse order) in the other languages.

To test our assumptions about efficiency and scalability we inferred a larger Tbox, subcategorisation frames and mappings using a pre-existing data set of verb frames for English encoded using the COMLEX subcategorisation frame inventory (Grishman et al., 1994). The linguistic resources for the application comprised a generative TAG grammar based on X-TAG (Doran et al., 1994) which we wrote ourselves, the CUV+ lexicon[3], and a pre-existing morphological generator for English (Hardcastle, 2007).

To test the performance of the generation process we used a set of randomly-generated Aboxes derived from the Tbox to produce texts of increasing size. For the purposes of testing we defined the size of an Abox as the total number of nodes and edges in the graph, which is the number of RDF triples required to represent it. Table 1 shows the size of the output text in sentences, the time taken to generate it in milliseconds, averaged over 5 runs, and the ratio of the time taken to the size of the output which shows linear scaling[4].

Size	Timing	Timing/Size
31	2	0.065
280	10	0.036
2,800	59	0.021
28,000	479	0.017

Table 1: The time, in milliseconds, taken to generate Aboxes of increasing size and the ratio of time taken to the size of the output.

To test the performance of the proving algorithm we ran the algorithm on a set of Tboxes of differing sizes. The smallest Tbox in Table 2 is the handcrafted proof-of-concept Tbox, the largest is the inferred Tbox described above, and the intermediate ones were pruned from the large, inferred Tbox at random cut points. The size of each Tbox is the total number of attribute-concept pairs which it defines. The table shows the time taken to run the prover from the root node of the Tbox with no starting syntactic context and the ratio of time taken to size, which shows linear scaling.

We tested the mechanics of the implementation of the prover through unit testing, and we tested the the design with a test suite of sample data. We performed white box tests by removing individual bindings from a set of mappings which we judged to be complete for the small handcrafted Tbox, and checked to ensure that each was highlighted by the prover. We performed black box tests by using a set of inferred mappings, judged by the prover to be complete, to generate from a large number of randomly structured Aboxes, drawn from our large inferred Tbox, and checked that the generation process never failed.

Size	Timing	Timing/Size
125	10	0.08
86,766	432	0.005
2,054,020	8,217	0.004
9,267,444	21,526	0.002

Table 2: The time, in milliseconds, taken to prove reliability for Tboxes of increasing size and the ratio of time taken to size.

We chose not to undertake a formal evaluation over and above the unit and sampling tests, because the accuracy of the prover is a function of the restricted domain of locality imposed by the system and of the recursive algorithm which depends on it. Instead we show that the prover is accurate by describing the parameters that guide search in generation and explaining why they can be exhaustively tested (see Section 5).

9 Conclusion

In this paper we presented a tactical generator which exploits a simplifying assumption that the output text will be restricted to controlled natural language to enforce a restricted domain of locality on search in generation. As a result, the generation process is fast and scales linearly, and furthermore the system is reliable, since we are able to perform a compile-time check of the data sources which drive the assignment of syntactic subcategorisations to the expression of each node in the input semantic graph.

The generator is most appropriate for applications which need to present small chunks of structured data as text on demand and in high volume. For example, information feeds such as local weather forecasts, traffic information, and tourist information or technical information that must be both machine-readable (for example because it is safety critical and requires consistency checking) and also human-readable (for example for an operator to make use of it) such as machine operator instructions, business process/protocol descriptions and medical orders.

[3]A publicly available lexicon for English available from the Oxford Text Archive

[4]In fact scaling is slightly sub-linear for this test and the test of the proving algorithm. In both cases that is because of caching within the framework to improve performance.

References

F. Baader, D. Calvanese, D. L. Mcguinness, D. Nardi, and P. F. Patel-Schneider, editors. 2003. *The Description Logic Handbook : Theory, Implementation and Applications*. Cambridge University Press.

J. Bateman, R. Kasper, J. Moore, and R. Whitney. 1989. A general organization of knowledge for natural language processing: The Penman Upper Model. Technical report, Information Sciences Institute, Marina del Rey, California.

T. Berners-Lee, J. Hendler, and O. Lassila. 2001. The Semantic Web. *Scientific American*, 284(5):34–43.

M. Candito and S. Kahane. 1998. Can the TAG derivation tree represent a semantic graph? An answer in the light of the Meaning-Text Theory. In *Proceedings of the Fourth Workshop on Tree-Adjoining Grammars and Related Frameworks*, Philadephia, USA.

R. Dale. 1989. Cooking up referring expressions. In *Proceedings of the 27th Annual Meeting of the Association for Computational Linguistics*, pages 68 – 75, Vancouver, Canada.

C. Doran, D. Egedia, B. Hockey, B. Srinivas, and M. Zaidel. 1994. XTAG system - a wide coverage grammar for English. In *Proceedings of the 15th International Conference on Computational Linguistics*, pages 922–928, Kyoto, Japan.

M. Fowler. 2004. Inversion of control containers and the dependency injection pattern `http://www.martinfowler.com/articles/injection.html`.

R. Grishman, C. McLeod, and A. Myers. 1994. Comlex Syntax: Building a Computational Lexicon. In *Proceedings of the The 15th International Conference on Computational Linguistics*, pages 268–272, Kyoto, Japan.

D. Hardcastle and R. Power. 2008. Generating Conceptually Aligned Texts. Technical Report 2008/06, The Open University, Milton Keynes, UK.

D. Hardcastle. 2007. Riddle posed by computer (6): The Computer Generation of Cryptic Crossword Clues. PhD thesis, University of London.

A. Hartley and C. Paris. 2001. Translation, controlled languages, generation. In E. Steiner and C. Yallop, editors, *Exploring Translation and Multilingual Text production*, pages 307–325. Mouton de Gruyter.

A. Joshi. 1987. The relevance of tree adjoining grammar to generation. In G. Kempen, editor, *Natural Language Generation: New Directions in Artificial Intelligence, Psychology, and Linguistics*. Kluwer.

O. Lassila and R. Swick. 1998. Resource Description Framework (RDF) model and syntax specification. W3C Working Draft WD-rdf-syntax-19981008.

C. Paris, K. Vander Linden, M. Fischer, A. Hartley, L. Pemberton, R. Power, and D. Scott. 1995. A support tool for writing multilingual instructions. In *Proceedings of the 14th International Joint Conference on Artificial Intelligence*, pages 1398–1404, Montreal, Canada.

R. Power and D. Scott. 1998. Multilingual authoring using feedback texts. In *Proceedings of the 17th International Conference on Computational Linguistics and 36th Annual Meeting of the Association for Computational Linguistics*, pages 1053–1059, Montreal, Canada.

R. Power, D. Scott, and N. Bouayad-Agha. 2003. Document structure. *Computational Linguistics*, 29(4):211–260.

Parallel Implementations of Word Alignment Tool

Qin Gao and **Stephan Vogel**
Language Technology Institution
School of Computer Science
Carnegie Mellon University
Pittsburgh, PA, 15213, USA
{qing, stephan.vogel}@cs.cmu.edu

Abstract

Training word alignment models on large corpora is a very time-consuming processes. This paper describes two parallel implementations of GIZA++ that accelerate this word alignment process. One of the implementations runs on computer clusters, the other runs on multi-processor system using multi-threading technology. Results show a near-linear speedup according to the number of CPUs used, and alignment quality is preserved.

1 Introduction

Training state-of-the-art phrase-based statistical machine translation (SMT) systems requires several steps. First, word alignment models are trained on the bilingual parallel training corpora. The most widely used tool to perform this training step is the well-known GIZA++(Och and Ney, 2003). The resulting word alignment is then used to extract phrase pairs and perhaps other information to be used in translation systems, such as block reordering models. Among the procedures, more than 2/3 of the time is consumed by word alignment (Koehn et al., 2007). Speeding up the word alignment step can dramatically reduces the overall training time, and in turn accelerates the development of SMT systems.

With the rapid development of computing hardware, multi-processor servers and clusters become widely available. With parallel computing, processing time (wall time) can often be cut down by one or two orders of magnitude. Tasks, which require several weeks on a single CPU machine may take only a few hours on a cluster. However, GIZA++ was designed to be single-process and single-thread. To make more efficient use of available computing resources and thereby speed up the training of our SMT system, we decided to modify GIZA++ so that it can run in parallel on multiple CPUs.

The word alignment models implemented in GIZA++, the so-called IBM (Brown et al., 1993) and HMM alignment models (Vogel et al., 1996) are typical implementation of the EM algorithm (Dempster et al., 1977). That is to say that each of these models run for a number of iterations. In each iteration it first calculates the best word alignment for each sentence pairs in the corpus, accumulating various counts, and then normalizes the counts to generate the model parameters for the next iteration. The word alignment stage is the most time-consuming part, especially when the size of training corpus is large. During the aligning stage, all sentences can be aligned independently of each other, as model parameters are only updated after all sentence pairs have been aligned. Making use of this property, the alignment procedure can be parallelized. The basic idea is to have multiple processes or threads aligning portions of corpus independently and then merge the counts and perform normalization.

The paper implements two parallelization methods. The PGIZA++ implementation, which is based on (Lin et al, 2006), uses multiple aligning processes. When all the processes finish, a master process starts to collect the counts and normalizes them to produce updated models. Child processes are then restarted for the new iteration. The PGIZA++ does not limit the number of CPUs being used, whereas it needs to transfer (in some cases) large amounts

Software Engineering, Testing, and Quality Assurance for Natural Language Processing, pages 49–57,
Columbus, Ohio, USA, June 2008. ©2008 Association for Computational Linguistics

of data between processes. Therefore its performance also depends on the speed of the network infrastructure. The MGIZA++ implementation, on the other hand, starts multiple threads on a common address space, and uses a mutual locking mechanism to synchronize the access to the memory. Although MGIZA++ can only utilize a single multi-processor computer, which limits the number of CPUs it can use, it avoids the overhead of slow network I/O. That makes it an equally efficient solution for many tasks. The two versions of alignment tools are available online at http://www.cs.cmu.edu/q̃ing/giza.

The paper will be organized as follows, section 2 provides the basic algorithm of GIZA++, and section 3 describes the PGIZA++ implementation. Section 4 presents the MGIZA++ implementation, followed by the profile and evaluation results of both systems in section 5. Finally, conclusion and future work are presented in section 6.

2 Outline of GIZA++

2.1 Statistical Word Alignment Models

GIZA++ aligns words based on statistical models. Given a source string $f_1^J = f_1, \cdots, f_j, \cdots, f_J$ and a target string $e_1^I = e_1, \cdots, e_i, \cdots, e_I$, an alignment $\mathcal{A}$ of the two strings is defined as(Och and Ney, 2003):

$$\mathcal{A} \subseteq \{(j,i) : j = 1, \cdots, J; i = 0, \cdots, I\} \quad (1)$$

in case that $i = 0$ in some $(j,i) \in \mathcal{A}$, it represents that the source word j aligns to an "empty" target word e_0.

In statistical world alignment, the probability of a source sentence given target sentence is written as:

$$P(f_1^J|e_1^I) = \sum_{a_1^J} P(f_1^J, a_1^J|e_1^I) \quad (2)$$

in which a_1^J denotes the alignment on the sentence pair. In order to express the probability in statistical way, several different parametric forms of $P(f_1^J, a_1^J|e_1^I) = p_\theta(f_1^J, a_1^J|e_1^I)$ have been proposed, and the parameters θ can be estimated using maximum likelihood estimation(MLE) on a training corpus(Och and Ney, 2003).

$$\hat{\theta} = \arg\max_\theta \prod_{s=1}^{S} \sum_a p_\theta(f_s, a|e_s) \quad (3)$$

The best alignment of the sentence pair,

$$\hat{a}_1^J = \arg\max_{a_1^J} p_{\hat{\theta}}(f_1^J, a_1^J|e_1^I) \quad (4)$$

is called Viterbi alignment.

2.2 Implementation of GIZA++

GIZA++ is an implementation of ML estimators for several statistical alignment models, including IBM Model 1 through 5 (Brown et al., 1993), HMM (Vogel et al., 1996) and Model 6 (Och and Ney, 2003).

Although IBM Model 5 and Model 6 are sophisticated, they do not give much improvement to alignment quality. IBM Model 2 has been shown to be inferior to the HMM alignment model in the sense of providing a good starting point for more complex models. (Och and Ney, 2003) So in this paper we focus on Model 1, HMM, Model 3 and 4.

When estimating the parameters, the EM (Dempster et al., 1977) algorithm is employed. In the E-step the counts for all the parameters are collected, and the counts are normalized in M-step. Figure 1 shows a high-level view of the procedure in GIZA++. Theoretically the E-step requires summing over all the alignments of one sentence pair, which could be $(I+1)^J$ alignments in total. While (Och and Ney, 2003) presents algorithm to implement counting over all the alignments for Model 1,2 and HMM, it is prohibitive to do that for Models 3 through 6. Therefore, the counts are only collected for a subset of alignments. For example, (Brown et al., 1993) suggested two different methods: using only the alignment with the maximum probability, the so-called Viterbi alignment, or generating a set of alignments by starting from the Viterbi alignment and making changes, which keep the alignment probability high. The later is called "pegging". (Al-Onaizan et al., 1999) proposed to use the neighbor alignments of the Viterbi alignment, and it yields good results with a minor speed overhead.

During training we starts from simple models use the simple models to bootstrap the more complex ones. Usually people use the following sequence: Model 1, HMM, Model 3 and finally Model 4. Table 1 lists all the parameter tables needed in each stage and their data structures[1]. Among these models, the

[1] In filename, *prefix* is a user specified parameter, and n is the number of the iteration.

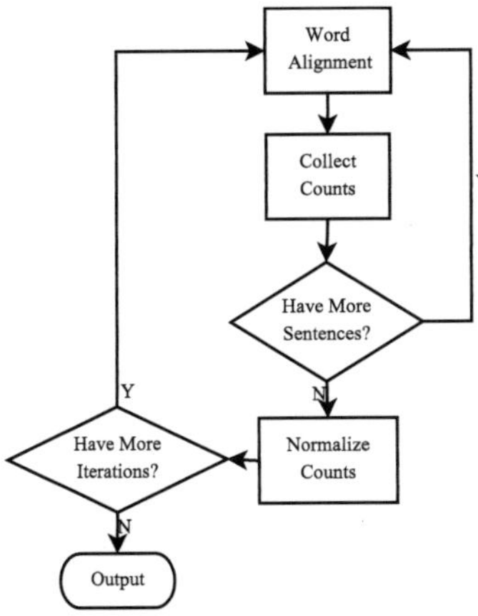

Figure 1: High-level algorithm of GIZA++

lexicon probability table (TTable) is the largest. It should contain all the $p(f_i, e_j)$ entries, which means the table will have an entry for every distinct source and target word pair f_i, e_j that co-occurs in at least one sentence pair in the corpus. However, to keep the size of this table manageable, low probability entries are pruned. Still, when training the alignment models on large corpora this statistical lexicon often consumes several giga bytes of memory.

The computation time of aligning a sentence pair obviously depends on the sentence length. E.g. for IBM 1 that alignment is $O(J * I)$, for the HMM alignment it is $O(J + I^2)$, with J the number of words in the source sentence and I the number of words in the target sentence. However, given that the maximum sentence length is fixed, the time complexity of the E-step grows linearly with the number of sentence pairs. The time needed to perform the M-step is dominated by re-normalizing the lexicon probabilities. The worst case time complexity is $O(|V_F| * |V_E|)$, where $|V_F|$ is the size of the source vocabulary and $|V_E|$ is the size of the target vocabulary. Therefore, the time complexity of the M-step is polynomial in the vocabulary size, which typically grows logarithmic in corpus size. As a result, the alignment stage consumes most of the overall processing time when the number of sentences is large.

Because the parameters are only updated during the M-step, it will be no difference in the result whether we perform the word alignment in the E-step sequentially or in parallel[2]. These characteristics make it possible to build parallel versions of GIZA++. Figure 2 shows the basic idea of parallel GIZA++.

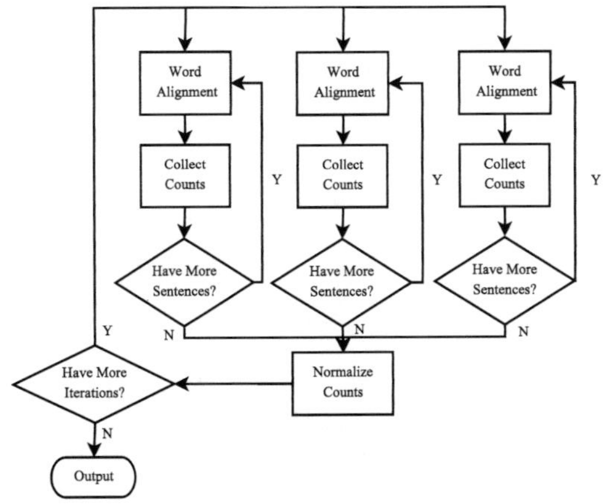

Figure 2: Basic idea of Parallel GIZA++

While working on the required modification to GIZA++ to run the alignment step in parallel we identified a bug, which needed to be fixed. When training the HMM model, the matrix for the HMM trellis will not be initialized if the target sentence has only one word. Therefore some random numbers are added to the counts. This bug will also crash the system when linking against *pthread* library. We observe different alignment and slightly lower perplexity after fixing the bug [3].

3 Multi-process version - PGIZA++

3.1 Overview

A natural idea of parallelizing GIZA++ is to separate the alignment and normalization procedures, and spawn multiple alignment processes. Each process aligns a chunk of the pre-partitioned corpus and outputs partial counts. A master process takes these counts and combines them, and produces the normalized model parameters for the next iteration. The architecture of PGIZA++ is shown in Figure 3.

[2] However, the rounding problem will make a small difference in the results even when processing the sentences sequentially, but in different order.

[3] The details of the bug can be found in: http://www.mail-archive.com/moses-support@mit.edu/msg00292.html

Model	Parameter tables	Filename	Description	Data structure
Model 1	TTable	*prefix*.t1.n	Lexicon Probability	Array of Array
HMM	TTable	*prefix*.thmm.n		
	ATable	*prefix*.ahmm.n	Align Table	4-D Array
	HMMTable	*prefix*.hhmm.n	HMM Jump	Map
Model 3/4	TTable	*prefix*.t3.n		
	ATable	*prefix*.a3.n	Align Table	
	NTable	*prefix*.n3.n	Fertility Table	2-D Array
	DTable	*prefix*.d3.n	Distortion Table	4-D Array
	pz	*prefix*.p0_3.n	Probability for null words p_0	Scalar
(Model 4 only)	D4Table	*prefix*.d4.n *prefix*.D4.n	Distortion Table for Model 4	Map

Table 1: Model tables created during training

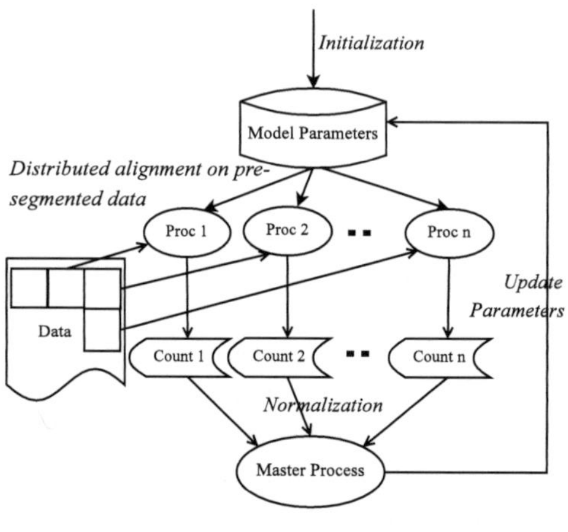

Figure 3: Architecture of PGIZA++

3.2 Implementation

3.2.1 I/O of the Parameter Tables

In order to ensure that the next iteration has the correct model, all the information that may affect the alignment needs to be stored and shared. It includes model files and statistics over the training corpus. Table 1 is a summary of tables used in each model.

Step	Without Pruning(MB)	With Pruning(MB)
Model 1, Step 1	1,273	494
HMM , Step 5	1,275	293
Model 4 , Step 3	1,280	129

Table 2: Comparison of the size of count tables for the lexicon probabilities

In addition to these models, the summation of "sentence weight" of the whole corpus should be stored. GIZA++ allows assigning a weight w_i for each sentence pair s_i sto indicate the number of occurrence of the sentence pair. The weight is normalized by $p_i = w_i / \sum_i w_i$, so that $\sum_i p_i = 1$. Then the p_i serves as a prior probability in the objective function. As each child processes only see a portion of training data, it is required to calculate and share the $\sum_i w_i$ among the children so the values can be consistent.

The tables and count tables of the lexicon probabilities (TTable) can be extremely large if not pruned before being written out. Pruning the count tables when writing them into a file will make the result slightly different. However, as we will see in Section 5, the difference does not hurt translation performance significantly. Table 2 shows the size of count tables written by each child process in an experiment with 10 million sentence pairs, remember there are more than 10 children writing the the count tables, and the master would have to read all these tables, the amount of I/O is significantly reduced by pruning the count tables.

3.2.2 Master Control Script

The other issue is the master control script. The script should be able to start processes in other nodes. Therefore the implementation varies according to the software environment. We implemented three versions of scripts based on secure shell, Condor (Thain et al., 2005) and Maui.

Also, the master must be notified when a child process finishes. In our implementation, we use signal files in the network file system. When the child process finishes, it will touch a predefined file in a shared folder. The script keeps watching the folder and when all the children have finished, the script runs the normalization process and then starts the next iteration.

3.3 Advantages and Disadvantages

One of the advantages of PGIZA++ is its scalability, it is not limited by the number of CPUs of a single machine. By adding more nodes, the alignment speed can be arbitrarily fast[4]. Also, by splitting the corpora into multiple segments, each child process only needs part of the lexicon, which saves memory. The other advantage is that it can adopt different resource management systems, such as Condor and Maui/Torque. By splitting the corpus into very small segments, and submitting them to a scheduler, we can get most out of clusters.

However, PGIZA++ also has significant drawbacks. First of all, each process needs to load the models of the previous iteration, and store the counts of the current step on shared storage. Therefore, I/O becomes a bottleneck, especially when the number of child processes is large. Also, the normalization procedure needs to read all the count files from network storage. As the number of child processes increases, the time spent on reading/writing will also increase. Given the fact that the I/O demand will not increase as fast as the size of corpus grows, PGIZA++ can only provide significant speed up when the size of each training corpus chunk is large enough so that the alignment time is significantly longer than normalization time.

Also, one obvious drawback of PGIZA++ is its complexity in setting up the environment. One has to write scripts specially for the scheduler/resource management software.

Balancing the load of each child process is another issue. If any one of the corpus chunks takes longer to complete, the master has to wait for it. In other words, the speed of PGIZA++ is actually determined by the slowest child process.

4 Multi-thread version - MGIZA++

4.1 Overview

Another implementation of parallelism is to run several alignment threads in a single process. The threads share the same address space, which means it can access the model parameters concurrently without any I/O overhead.

[4]The normalization process will be slower when the number of nodes increases

The architecture of MGIZA++ is shown in Figure 4.

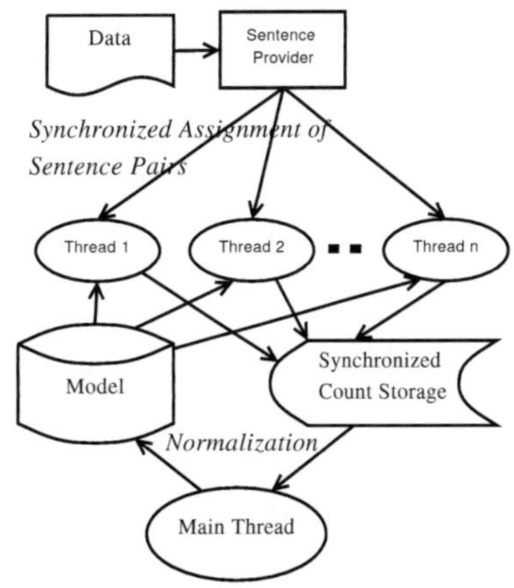

Figure 4: Architecture of MGIZA++

4.2 Implementation

The main thread spawns a number of threads, using the same entry function. Each thread will ask a provider for the next sentence pair. The sentence provider is synchronized. The request of sentences are queued, and each sentence pair is guaranteed to be assigned to only one thread.

The threads do alignment in their own stacks, and read required probabilities from global parameter tables, such as the TTable, which reside on the heap. Because no update on these global tables will be performed during this stage, the reading can be concurrent. After aligning the sentence pairs, the counts need to be collected. For HMMTable and D4Table, which use maps as their data structure, we cannot allow concurrent read/write to the table, because the map structure may be changed when inserting a new entry. So we must either put mutual locks to postpone reading until writing is complete, or duplicate the tables for each thread and merge them afterwards. Locking can be very inefficient because it may block other threads, so the duplicate/merge method is a much better solution. However, for the TTable the size is too large to have multiple copies. Instead, we put a lock on every target word, so only when two thread try to write counts for the same target word will a collisions happen. We also have to put mutual locks on the accumulators used to calculate the alignment perplexity.

Table	Synchronizations Method
TTable	Write lock on every target words
ATable	Duplicate/Merge
HMMTable	Duplicate/Merge
DTable	Duplicate/Merge
NTable	Duplicate/Merge
D4Table	Duplicate /Merge
Perplexity	Mutual lock

Table 3: Synchronizations for tables in MGIZA++

Each thread outputs the alignment into its own output file. Sentences in these files are not in sequential order. Therefore, we cannot simply concatenate them but rather have to merge them according to the sentence id.

4.3 Advantages and Disadvantages

Because all the threads within a process share the same address space, no data needs to be transferred, which saves the I/O time significantly. MGIZA++ is more resource-thrifty comparing to PGIZA++, it do not need to load copies of models into memory.

In contrast to PGIZA++, MGIZA++ has a much simpler interface and can be treated as a drop-in replacement for GIZA++, except that one needs to run a script to merge the final alignment files. This property makes it very simple to integrate MGIZA++ into machine translation packages, such as Moses(Koehn et al., 2007).

One major disadvantage of MGIZA++ is also obvious: lack of scalability. Accelerating is limited by the number of CPUs the node has. Compared to PGIZA++ on the speed-up factor by each additional CPU, MGIZA++ also shows some deficiency. Due to the need for synchronization, there are always some CPU time wasted in waiting.

5 Experiments

5.1 Experiments on PGIZA++

For PGIZA++ we performed training on an Chinese-English translation task. The dataset consists of approximately 10 million sentence pairs with 231 million Chinese words and 258 million English words. We ran both GIZA++ and PGIZA++ on the same training corpus with the same parameters, then ran Pharaoh phrase extraction on the resulting alignments. Finally, we tuned our translation systems on the NIST MT03 test set and evaluate them on NIST MT06 test set. The experiment was performed on a cluster of several Xeon CPUs, the storage of corpora and models are on a central NFS server. The PGIZA++ uses Condor as its scheduler, splitting the training data into 30 fragments, and ran training in both direction (Ch-En, En-Ch) concurrently. The scheduler assigns 11 CPUs on average to the tasks. We ran 5 iterations of Model 1 training, 5 iteration of HMM, 3 Model 3 iterations and 3 Model 4 iterations. To compare the performance of system, we recorded the total training time and the BLEU score, which is a standard automatic measurement of the translation quality(Papineni et al., 2002). The training time and BLEU scores are shown in Table 4: [5]

	Running Time	(TUNE) MT03	(TEST) MT06	CPUs
GIZA++	169h	32.34	29.43	2
PGIZA++	39h	32.20	30.14	11

Table 4: Comparison of GIZA++ and PGIZA++

The results show similar BLEU scores when using GIZA++ and PGIZA++, and a 4 times speed up.

Also, we calculated the time used in normalization. The average time of each normalization step is shown in Table 5.

	Per-iteration (Avg)	Total
Model 1	47.0min	235min (3.9h)
HMM	31.8min	159min (2.6h)
Model 3/4	25.2 min	151min (2.5h)

Table 5: Normalization time in each stage

As we can see, if we rule out the time spent in normalization, the speed up is almost linear. Higher order models require less time in the normalization step mainly due to the fact that the lexicon becomes smaller and smaller with each models (see Table 2. PGIZA++, in small amount of data,

5.2 Experiment on MGIZA++

Because MGIZA++ is more convenient to integrate into other packages, we modified the Moses system to use MGIZA++. We use the Europal English-Spanish dataset as training data, which contains 900 thousand sentence pairs, 20 million English words and 20 million Spanish words. We trained the

[5] All the BLEU scores in the paper are case insensitive.

English-to-Spanish system, and tuned the system on two datasets, the WSMT 2006 Europal test set (TUNE1) and the WSMT news commentary devtest set 2007 (TUNE2). Then we used the first parameter set to decode WSMT 2006 Europal test set (TEST1) and used the second on WSMT news commentary test set 2007 (TEST2)[6]. Table 6 shows the comparison of BLEU scores of both systems. listed in Table 6:

	TUNE1	TEST1	TUNE2	TEST2
GIZA++	33.00	32.21	31.84	30.56
MGIZA++	32.74	32.26	31.35	30.63

Table 6: BLEU Score of GIZA++ and MGIZA++

Note that when decoding using the phrase table resulting from training with MGIZA++, we used the parameter tuned for a phrase table generated from GIZA++ alignment, which may be the cause of lower BLEU score in the tuning set. However, the major difference in the training comes from fixing the HMM bug in GIZA++, as mentioned before.

To profile the speed of the system according to the number of CPUs it use, we ran MGIZA++ on 1, 2 and 4 CPUs of the same speed. When it runs on 1 CPU, the speed is the same as for the original GIZA++. Table 7 and Figure 5 show the running time of each stage:

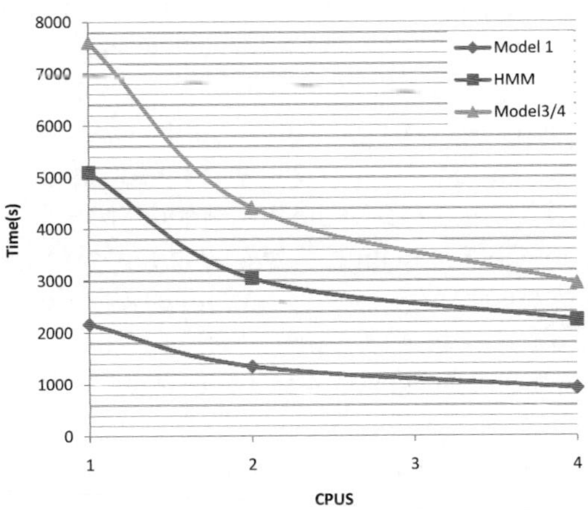

Figure 5: Speed up of MGIZA++

When using 4 CPUs, the system uses only 41% time comparing to one thread. Comparing to PGIZA++, MGIZA++ does not have as high an acceleration rate. That is mainly because of the required locking mechanism. However the acceleration is also significant, especially for small training corpora, as we will see in next experiment.

CPUs	M1(s)	HMM(s)	M3,M4(s)	Total(s)
1	2167	5101	7615	14913
2	1352 (62%)	3049 (59%)	4418 (58%)	8854 (59%)
4	928 (43%)	2240 (44%)	2947 (38%)	6140 (41%)

Table 7: Speed of MGIZA++

5.3 Comparison of MGIZA++ and PGIZA++

In order to compare the acceleration rate of PGIZA++ and MGIZA++, we also ran PGIZA++ in the same dataset as described in the previous section with 4 children. To avoid the delay of starting the children processes, we chose to use ssh to start remote tasks directly, instead of using schedulers. The results are listed in Table 8.

	M1(s)	HMM(s)	M3,M4(s)	Total(s)
MGIZA+1CPU	2167	5101	7615	14913
MGIZA+4CPUs	928	2240	2947	6140
PGIZA+4Nodes	3719	4324	4920	12963

Table 8: Speed of PGIZA++ on Small Corpus

There is nearly no speed-up observed, and in Model 1 training, we observe a loss in the speed. Again, by investigating the time spent in normalization, the phenomenon can be explained (Table 9):

Even after ruling out the normalization time, the speed up factor is smaller than MGIZA++. That is because of reading models when child processes start and writing models when child processes finish.

From the experiment we can conclude that PGIZA++ is more suited to train on large corpora than on small or moderate size corpora. It is also important to determine whether to use PGIZA++ rather than MGIZA++ according to the speed of network storage infrastructure.

5.4 Difference in Alignment

To compare the difference in final Viterbi alignment output, we counted the number of sentences that have different alignments in these systems. We use

[6] http://www.statmt.org/wmt08/shared-task.html

	Per-iteration (Avg)	Total
Model 1	8.4min	41min (0.68h)
HMM	7.2min	36min (0.60h)
Model 3/4	5.7 min	34min (0.57h)
Total		111min (1.85h)

Table 9: Normalization time in each stage : small data

GIZA++ with the bug fixed as the reference. The results of all other systems are listed in Table 10:

	Diff Lines	Diff Percent
GIZA++(origin)	100,848	10.19%
MGIZA++(4CPU)	189	0.019%
PGIZA++(4Nodes)	18,453	1.86%

Table 10: Difference in Viterbi alignment (GIZA++ with the bug fixed as reference)

From the comparison we can see that PGIZA++ has larger difference in the generated alignment. That is partially because of the pruning on count tables.

To also compare the alignment score in the different systems. For each sentence pair $i = 1, 2, \cdots, N$, assume two systems b and c have Viterbi alignment scores S_i^b, S_i^c. We define the residual $\mathcal{R}$ as:

$$\mathcal{R} = 2\sum_i \left(\frac{|S_i^b - S_i^c|}{(S_i^b + S_i^c)} \right) /N \qquad (5)$$

The residuals of the three systems are listed in Table 11. The residual result shows that the MGIZA++ has a very small (less than 0.2%) difference in alignment scores, while PGIZA++ has a larger residual.

The results of experiments show the efficiency and also the fidelity of the alignment generated by the two versions of parallel GIZA++. However, there are still small differences in the final alignment result, especially for PGIZA++. Therefore, one should consider which version to choose when building systems. Generally speaking, MGIZA++ provides smoother integration into other packages: easy to set up and also more precise. PGIZA++ will not perform as good as MGIZA++ on small-size corpora. However, PGIZA++ has good performance on large data, and should be considered when building very large scale systems.

6 Conclusion

The paper describes two parallel implementations of the well-known and widely used word alignment tool GIZA++. PGIZA++ does alignment on a number of independent processes, uses network file system to collect counts, and performs normalization by a master process. MGIZA++ uses a multi-threading mechanism to utilize multiple cores and avoid network transportation. The experiments show that the two implementation produces similar results with original GIZA++, but lead to a significant speed-up in the training process.

	$\mathcal{R}$
GIZA++(origin)	0.6503
MGIZA++(4CPU)	0.0017
PGIZA++(4Nodes)	0.0371

Table 11: Residual in Viterbi alignment scores (GIZA++ with the bug fixed as reference)

With compatible interface, MGIZA++ is suitable for a drop-in replacement for GIZA++, while PGIZA++ can utilize huge computation resources, which is suitable for building large scale systems that cannot be built using a single machine.

However, improvements can be made on both versions. First, a combination of the two implementation is reasonable, i.e. running multi-threaded child processes inside PGIZA++'s architecture. This could reduce the I/O significantly when using the same number of CPUs. Secondly, the mechanism of assigning sentence pairs to the child processes can be improved in PGIZA++. A server can take responsibility to assign sentence pairs to available child processes dynamically. This would avoid wasting any computation resource by waiting for other processes to finish. Finally, the huge model files, which are responsible for a high I/O volume can be reduced by using binary formats. A first implementation of a simple binary format for the TTable resulted in files only about 1/3 in size on disk compared to the plain text format.

The recent development of MapReduce framework shows its capability to parallelize a variety of machine learning algorithms, and we are attempting to port word alignment tools to this framework. Currently, the problems to be addressed is the I/O bottlenecks and memory usage, and an attempt to use distributed structured storage such as HyperTable to enable fast access to large tables and also performing filtering on the tables to alleviate the memory issue.

References

Arthur Dempster, Nan Laird, and Donald Rubin. 1977. *Maximum Likelihood From Incomplete Data via the EM Algorithm.* Journal of the Royal Statistical Society, Series B, 39(1):138

Douglas Thain, Todd Tannenbaum, and Miron Livny. 2005. *Distributed Computing in Practice: The Condor Experience.* Concurrency and Computation: Practice and Experience, 17(2-4):323-356

Franz Josef Och and Hermann Ney. 2003. *A Systematic Comparison of Various Statistical Alignment Models.* Computational Linguistics, 29(1):19-51

Philipp Koehn, Hieu Hoang, Alexandra Birch, Chris Callison-Burch, Marcello Federico, Nicola Bertoldi, Brooke Cowan, Wade Shen, Christine Moran, Richard Zens, Chris Dyer, Ondrej Bojar, Alexandra Constantin, Evan Herbst. 2007. *Moses: Open Source Toolkit for Statistical Machine Translation.* ACL 2007, Demonstration Session, Prague, Czech Republic

Peter F. Brown, Stephan A. Della Pietra, Vincent J. Della Pietra, Robert L. Mercer. 1993. *The Mathematics of Statistical Machine Translation: Parameter Estimation.* Computational Linguistics, 19(2):263-311

Stephan Vogel, Hermann Ney and Christoph Tillmann. 1996. *HMM-based Word Alignment in Statistical Translation.* In COLING '96: The 16th International Conference on Computational Linguistics, pp. 836-841, Copenhagen, Denmark.

Xiaojun Lin, Xinhao Wang and Xihong Wu. 2006. *NLMP System Description for the 2006 NIST MT Evaluation.* NIST 2006 Machine Translation Evaluation

Yaser Al-Onaizan, Jan Curin, Michael Jahr, Kevin Knight, John D. Lafferty, I. Dan Melamed, David Purdy, Franz J. Och, Noah A. Smith and David Yarowsky. 1999. *Statistical Machine Translation.* Final Report JHU Workshop, Available at http://www.clsp.jhu.edu/ws99/projects/mt/final_report/mt-final-reports.ps

Kishore Papineni, Salim Roukos, Todd Ward and Wei-Jing Zhu 2002. *BLEU: a Method for Automatic Evaluation of machine translation.* Proc. of the 40th Annual Conf. of the Association for Computational Linguistics (ACL 02), pp. 311-318, Philadelphia, PA

Design of the Moses Decoder for Statistical Machine Translation

Hieu Hoang
University of Edinburgh
h.hoang@sms.ed.ac.uk

Philipp Koehn
University of Edinburgh
pkoehn@inf.ed.ac.uk

Abstract

We present a description of the implementation of the open source decoder for statistical machine translation which has become popular with many researchers in SMT research. The goal of the project is to create an open, high quality phrase-based decoder which can reduce the time and barrier to entry for researchers wishing to do SMT research. We discuss the major design objective for the Moses decoder, its performance relative to other SMT decoders, and the steps we are taking to ensure that its success will continue.

1 Motivation

Phrase-based translation has been one of the major advances in statistical machine translation (Brown et al. 1990) in recent years and is currently one of the techniques which can claim to be state-of-the-art in machine translation. Phrase-based models are a development of the word based models as exemplified by the (Brown et al. 1990). In phrase-based translation, contiguous segments of words in the input sentence are mapped to contiguous segments of words in the output sentence.

In SMT, we are given a source language sentence, s, which is to be translated into a target language sentence, t. The goal of machine translation is to find the translation, $\hat{t}$, which is defined as:

$$\hat{t} = \arg\max_t \, p(t \mid s)$$

where $p(t \mid s)$ is the probability model. The argmax implies a search for the best translation $\hat{t}$ in the space of possible translations t. This search is the task of the decoder, which we will concentrate on in this paper.

There have been numerous implementations of phrase-based decoders for SMT prior to our work. Early systems such as the Alignment Template System (ATS) (Och and Ney 2004) and Pharaoh (Koehn 2004) were widely used and accepted by the research community. ATS is perhaps the cross-over system, in that word classes were translated as phrases but the surface words were translated word by word. Pharaoh substituted the word classes with surface words, thereby discarding the use of word classes in decoding altogether.

There has been other phrase-based decoders such as PORTAGE (Sadat et al. 2005), Phramer (Olteanu et al. 2006), the MITLL/AFRL system (Shen et al. 2005), ITC-irst (Bertoldi et al. 2004), Ramses/Mood (Patry et al. 2006) to name but a few. Other researchers such as (Kumar and Byrne 2003) have also used weighted finite state transducers but they have more difficulty modeling reordering.

Many early systems came with restrictive licenses; ATS has never been publicly released, Pharaoh was released in 2003 as a pre-compiled binary with documentation. This severely limited the extent to which other researchers can study and enhance the decoder. Without access to the decoder source code research was generally restricted to altering the input, augmenting it with extra information, or modifying the output or re-ranking the n-best list output.

The main contribution of this paper is to show how we have created an extensible decoder, has acceptable run time performance compared to similar systems, and the ease of use and development that has made it the preferred choice for researchers looking for a phrase-based SMT decoder.

Software Engineering, Testing, and Quality Assurance for Natural Language Processing, pages 58–65,
Columbus, Ohio, USA, June 2008. ©2008 Association for Computational Linguistics

As an indication of the take-up of the Moses toolkit, out of over 20 competing teams at the recent IWSLT 2007 conference[1], half used Moses.

As an indication of the extensibility of the decoder, there are currently four language model implementations which has been integrated with the decoder by various researchers. In addition, the framework exists to integrate language models, such as those described in (Bilmes and Kirchhoff 2003), which takes advantage of the factored representation within Moses.

It is noted that Mood/Ramses also supports multiple LM implementations, an internally developed language model, in additional to SRILM, to overcome the latter's licensing restrictions.

In addition, there are two built-in phrase table implementations, one which loads all data into memory for fast decoding, and a binary phrase table as described in (Zens and Ney 2007) which loads on demand to conserve memory usage.

The Moses decoder has the ability to accept simple sentence input, confusion network or lattice networks, in common with SMT decoders such as the MITLL/AFRL or ITC-irst systems. The decoder also produces diverse types of output, ranging from 1-best, n-best lists and word lattices.

2 Comparison with other projects

The Moses decoder is designed within a strict modular and object-oriented framework for easy maintainability and extensibility.

In designing the decoder, we modeled the software design methodology and aims on some research-oriented software libraries outside of the SMT and NLP field which is open source, written in C++, have a large and diverse user-base, have succeeded in becoming the industry norm in their field.

Specifically, we modeled the software on the CGAL library (Fabri et al. 2000), used in computational geometry, and DCMTK (Eichelberg et al. 2004) library used in medical imaging. We believe they set good examples of the standards that we should follow.

However, there are differences between our project and CGAL or DCMTK.

The first difference is project size, for example, whereas CGAL consists of over 500,000 lines of code and multiple libraries and example program, the Moses decoder consists of 20,000 lines in 2 libraries. The difference is scale makes implementing some steps in the development life cycle impractical or unnecessary. For example, functionality specification before implementation was described for CGAL and is typical of large projects but would have been cumbersome for Moses.

Secondly, the aims of Moses and these projects are different. The goal of the CGAL project is to *'make…computational geometry available for industrial application'*[2].

Both CGAL and DCMTK are used extensively in commercial applications. Therefore, issues such robustness, cross-platform compatibility and ease-of-use are predominant for these projects.

Commercialization is not an aim of the Moses project but we believe these issues are still as important as they affect the usability and uptake of the system. Therefore, the Moses decoder was built to address these issues without compromising the academic priorities of the project.

Thirdly, the correct implementation is easier to decide in libraries such as CGAL as the algorithms are closely specified by the mathematical specification, therefore, testing and specification writing is more prevalent and easier than in Moses. For DCMTK, the medical imaging standards and protocols offers a clear guide for implementation. By contrast, the function of an SMT decoder is search for which there are no correct implementation, we can only measure its performance relative to previous versions and other similar decoders.

These differences are minor compared to the similarities Moses has to CGAL and DCMTK, and indeed, to any well developed software project. Design goals such as robustness, flexibility, ease of use and efficiency are commonality that we share and which we will discuss in more detail in the next section.

As a contrast to CGAL and DCMTK whose design we would like to emulate, we also looked at a project within the NLP field which contains certain aspect in the design we would like to avoid.

GIZA++ (Och and Ney 2003) is a very popular system within SMT for creating word alignment from parallel corpus, in fact, the Moses training scripts uses it. The system was release under the GPL open source license. However, its lack of

[1] http://iwslt07.oitc.it/menu/program.html

[2] http://cordis.europa.eu/esprit/src/21957.htm

clear design, documentation and obscure coding style makes it difficult for other researcher to contribute or extend the system. For a long time, it couldn't even be compiled on modern GCC compilers. Other systems which seeks to improve word alignment and segmentation, such as MTTK (Deng et al. 2006), have been created to replace GIZA++.

3 Design Goals

We decided to develop the Moses decoder as a C++ library.

We steered clear of scripting languages for performance reasons and the fact they often offer even less in the way of cross-platform compatibility. Java was also avoided for performance reasons but it's rich library and multi-platform support would have been useful.

We note that Hiero (Chiang 2005) is written in a scripting language with performance critical components rewritten in a compiled language. This is not the approach we considered as we believed it would have raised the complexity and reduce reliability of the project having to develop (and debug) in two languages and managing the interface between them. We also note that the LinearB and Phramer decoders are implemented in Java and have reported significantly worse run time speeds, (Olteanu et al. 2006).

C++ can be inelegant and difficult for inexperienced developers but using other object oriented language such as Smalltalk or C# was out of the question as they lack acceptance within the MT research community.

3.1 Comparable Performance

The Pharaoh decoder (Koehn 2004) represented the state-of-the-art in phrase-based decoders prior to the introduction of Moses. Moses was designed to supersede Pharaoh in performance and functionality. Moses was used as the basis for the JHU Workshop (Koehn et al. 2006) on Factored Machine Translation where it was extensively enhanced; we capitalized on the experience of colleagues at the workshop and used Pharaoh as the baseline during development to ensure that we obtain comparable performance. Table 1 shows the comparison of the translation performance of Pharaoh and Moses for a typical decoding of 2000 sentence trained on the news-commentary corpus[3]. We also include Phramer as an example of a Java-based decoder. Due to improvements in the search algorithm, Moses can slightly outperform Pharaoh on most tasks, which was confirmed by (Shen et al. 2007).

Table 1 Comparison with pharaoh & Phramer for a typical fr-en translation of 2000 sentences

	Time taken	Peak memory usage	BLEU
Pharaoh	99min	46MB	19.57
Moses	69min	154MB	19.57
Moses, with load on-demand PT & LM	102min	239MB	19.57
Phramer	649min	1218MB	19.44

In addition, most of the functionality of Pharaoh has been replicated.

3.2 Integration of Word-Level Factors

The Moses decoder isn't purely a clone of Pharaoh, it was created to conduct research into word-level factors in phrase-base MT. Whereas traditional, non-factored SMT typically deals only with the surface form of words, factored translation models augments different factors, such as POS tags or lemma, into source and target sentences to improve translation. This transforms the representation of a word from a string to a vector of strings, and a phrase or sentence from a sequence of words to a sequence of vectors. Such a change to the basic data structure of a decoder propagated throughout the rest of the system, therefore, it was simpler to build the Moses decoder from scratch rather than extend an existing decoder such as Pharaoh.

Some research into factored machine translation has been published by (Koehn and Hoang 2007).

3.3 Flexibility

Flexibility is an important software design goal which will enable researchers to extend the use of the Moses decoders to tasks that were not originally envisioned.

Following (Fabri et al. 2000), we identify four sub-issues which affects flexibility:

i. Modularity

[3] http://www.statmt.org/wmt07/shared-task.html

ii. Adaptability
iii. Extensibility
iv. Openness

3.4 Modularity

Firstly, software modularity enables developers to work on one component of the decoder without affecting other components. A modular design reduces the learning curve for developers by shielding them from having to understand the entire system if they are only developing a specific part.

Modularity also assists in the re-using of components by separating the implementation details from the module interface.

Moses takes advantage of C++ support for object-oriented and generic programming to enable modularity.

In keeping with the extensible design of CGAL and DCMTK, the core of the decoder is compiled as a static library which can interact with other components through a well-defined API. The simple application which currently comes with the decoder enables users to use the system via the command line and also provides an example of the API.

Therefore, the current typical compilation of the decoder would combine the libraries from IRSTLM, SRILM, Moses, and moses-cmd to create a binary executable.

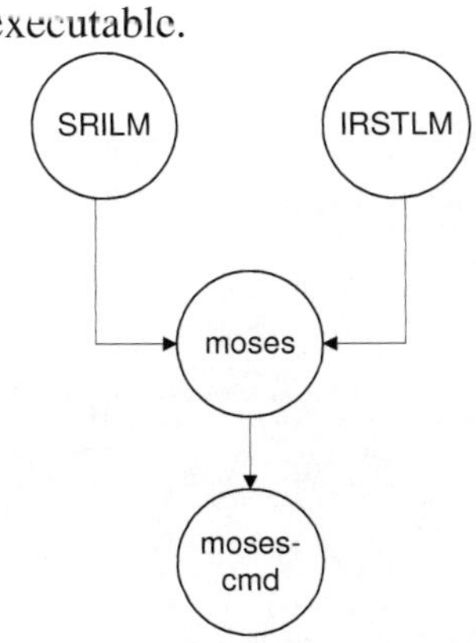

Figure 1 Project Dependencies

Any of these libraries can be dropped or replaced with other components with the same API.

We detail some examples of the object-oriented design of Moses below.

The input into the decoder can be one of three types: a simple string (sentence), a confusion network or a lattice network, Figure 2.

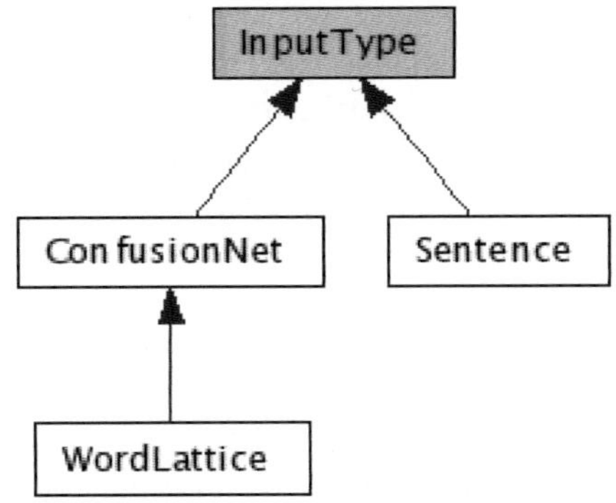

Figure 2 Input Types

Language models are abstracted to enable different implementations to be used and provide a framework for more complex models such as factored LM and the Bloom filter language model (Talbot and Osborne 2007). Similarly, phrase tables are abstracted to provide support for multiple implementations.

Each component model which contributes to the log-linear hypothesis score inherits from the ScoreProducer base class, Figure 3.

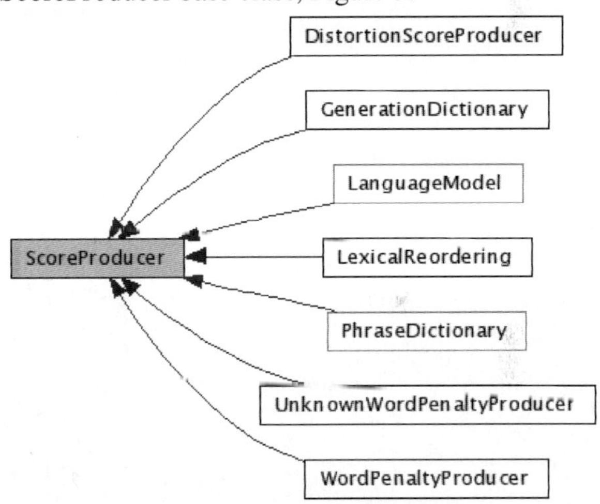

Figure 3 Score Producer

The Moses library provide a simple API whose main entry point is the class

```
Manager
```

This class is instantiated in the client application, moses-cmd in our case. Each input is decoded by calling the class method below:

```
ProcessSentence()
```

3.5 Adaptability

Phrase-based SMT is a fast moving research field where virtually all aspects of the theory are still being explored and implementations can be improved. The Moses decoder has to be amenable to researchers to adapt any component of the decoder in ways that perhaps wasn't foreseen in the original implementation.

Certainly, modularity plays an important part in this but it can also have the opposite effect of allowing obtuse or badly written implementation to hide behind the API, reducing the ability for researchers to question, investigate or extend. As a voluntary project, there is limited power to enforce good implementation and it would be difficult not to accept added functionality.

However, we use coding standards and designs during the development of the decoder that we hope makes the task of working with Moses easier for developers, and that they will continue to use those standards to uphold the clarity of the code.

These coding standards include:

i. strict object-oriented design
ii. descriptive variable, class, object and function names
iii. consistent indentation
iv. use of STL containers
v. implementation of STL-compatible iterators for internal container classes.

The source code for the Moses decoder has contributions from a number of developers in the last two years, Figure 4, including four developers who have made significant contributions but were not in the original JHU Workshop. However, code clarity has, by-and-large, remained intact.

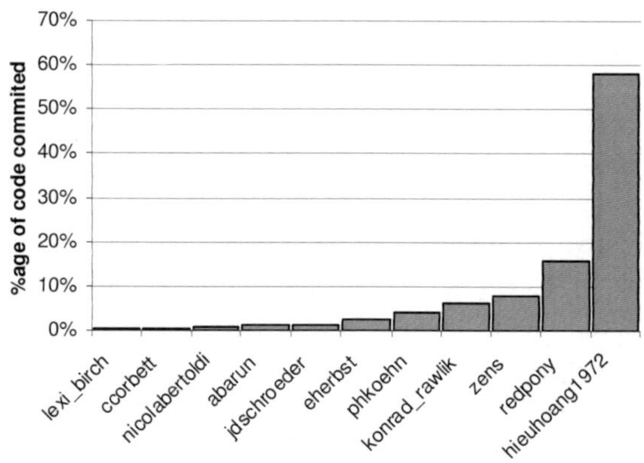

Figure 4 Code committed

We do not know how the decoder will be changed in future, nor do we know where and by whom it will be used. Moses is first and foremost an academic project but that doesn't exclude its use in commercial applications.

We also believe that it will be useful as a teaching tool for computational linguists, machine translation researchers or general computer science students. It is important with such a diverse potential user base, with widely varying degrees of C++ and programming experience, that we make the development and use of Moses as easy as possible, without imposing a significant burden on advanced users.

We would like to lower the learning curve by letting users use Moses in an environment and tools where they are most comfortable with. Therefore, the Moses decoder is operating system and compiler neutral. It is known to run on Windows (natively, or with Cygwin), Linux 32 and 64 bits, Mac OSX and OpenBSD. It is known to be compileable with modern gcc compilers, Visual Studio.net, Intel C++ for both Linux and Windows. We encourage the use of modern graphical integrated development environments (IDE) for Moses and include project files for Visual Studio, Eclipse and XCode, in addition to conventional makefiles.

We note that almost half of the source code downloads for the Moses toolkit from Sourceforge are for the non-Unix version, and that 58% of the visitors to the Moses website uses Windows, Figure 5.

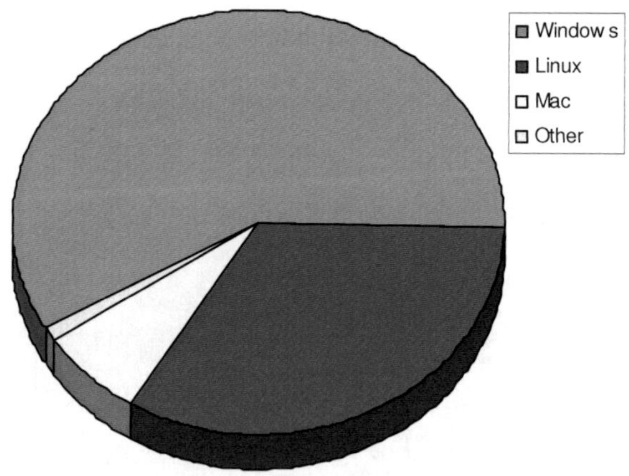

Figure 5 OS of Moses website visitors

This heterogeneous approach allows developers who have previously been excluded to participate within the SMT community and strengthens the decoder by allowing people of different backgrounds to apply their skills. This is of particular concern to us as we are attempting to integrate linguistic information into machine translation with factored decoding.

It also enables best-of-breed tools to be bought to the development of the decoder, regardless of platform. For example, we use both open source and commercial tools on Linux and Windows to track down memory issues, as well as performance profilers. This greatly enhances the efficiency of development and the reliability of the decoder.

Other NLP libraries, such as SRILM (Stolcke 2002) can be compiled and executed under multiple platforms but its development are very much Unix-centric so requires porting tools for non-Unix platforms. We believe the platform and compiler agnostic approach is unique for a major open source C++ project within recent NLP history.

3.6 Openness

An important reason for initiating the Moses project was the need to create a competitive decoder which could be extended with factors, as well as other advances in phrase-based machine translation. It is open source to enable other researchers to extend a state-of-the-art decoder without having to recreate what we have already built.

The decoder was improved at the JHU Workshop by a number of researchers so it needed to be flexible from the beginning. From this experience, we realize that releasing the source code is not enough. The decoder must be written and structured in a clear way to enable other researchers to contribute to the project.

Aside from the legalese of releasing the source code under an open source license, we believe that open source also means the source code is clear and accessible to allow others to examine, critique and contribute. Coding standards aimed at source code clarity and support for modern tools backs this goal.

Documentation of the algorithms used, and of the source code are also essential to allow others to understand the details of the decoder. Every class and function in the Moses decoder is commented in a Doxygen compatible format, HTML documents and figures, such as those in Figure 2 and Figure 3, are generated automatically from these comments and accessible via the Web[4].

Development is done through a source control system and all code changes are open to inspection. We encourage and enable all developers to use and extend Moses and feed back improvements. However, to ensure that the performance of the decoder is maintained and that changes to the decoder doesn't break existing setups, we maintain certain controls over the commit process.

There is a regression test suite which should be passed before any code can be committed to ensure that unintended divergence haven't crept in. A framework exists for creation of regression tests, developers who add new functionality to the decoder are encouraged to create additional tests to ensure that their functionality will work in future.

However, no amount of automated testing can be exhaustive. New committers are subject to peer review by a more experience contributor before the code is committed, and before the contributor is granted write access to the source control system. Also, code commits are monitored via email notifications to a public mailing list.

These measures add a little overhead to the development process this is necessary to maintain the quality of the system and assure to users and developers.

We have benefited from the examples of sound software engineering principles set by the CGAL and DCMTK project and hope that we will emulate their success by bringing these engineering principles into NLP. In contrast to the 'abandonware' status of GIZA++, both CGAL and DCMTK are still being developed.

4 Supporting Infrastructure

Other factors have contributed to the wide adoption of Moses.

4.1 'One-Stop Shop' for Phrase-Based SMT

The Moses project encompasses the decoder and many of the other components necessary to create a translation system which were previously available separately. These include scripts for creating alignments from a parallel corpus, creating phrase tables and language models, binarizing phrase tables, scripts for weight optimization using MERT (Och 2003), and testing scripts.

Steps such as MERT and testing which are CPU intensive have been re-engineered to run in parallel using Sun Grid Engine.

All scripts have also been extended for factored translation.

[4] http://www.statmt.org/moses/html/

4.2 Ongoing support

We assist in the adoption of Moses by offering ongoing support to users and developers through the support mailing list[5]. Questions relating to Moses, phrase-based translation or machine translation in general are often asked, and usually answered. The archived emails are publicly available and searchable, and have become an important knowledge source for the community.

The mailing list popularity has been steadily increasing since its inception, Figure 6, and is now the most popular mailing list for machine translation, based on volume.

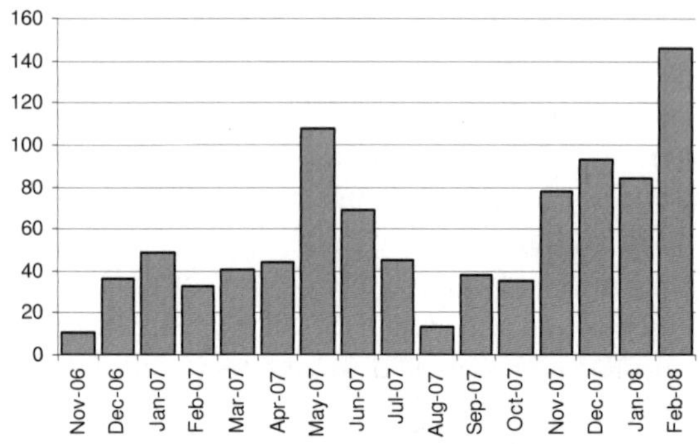

Figure 6 Emails to Moses support mailing list

5 Future Work

There has been some important developments in phrase-based translation in recent years, including the hierarchical phrase-based model as described in (Chiang 2005). Research have also been made into alternatives to the current log-linear scoring model such as discriminative models with millions of features (Liang et al. 2006), or kernel based models (Wang et al. 2007).

From a software engineering point of view, these improvements would require fundamental changes to the structure if they were to be implemented into Moses.

We are also interested in seeing the Moses decoder employed in search tasks outside of machine translation; Moses has been used for OCR correction, recasing, and transliteration.

Other improvements such as smaller, faster, more efficient phrase tables are also welcomed.

Lastly, we would like to see the training and tuning scripts re-engineered to the same modular design as the decoder. The future direction of the Moses decoder requires even more complex models which are already stretching the current script implementation to the limit of adaptability and reliability.

6 Conclusion

We have applied the sound software engineering principles and design to the implementation of the Moses decoder which has enabled other researchers to use and extend its functionality. We believe this has been a major factor for the widespread adoption of Moses within the SMT community. We hope that the design of the decoder will enable it to maintain it leading edge status into the future.

Acknowledgements

This work was supported in part under the GALE program of the Defense Advanced Research Projects Agency, Contract No. HR0011-06-C-0022 and in part under the EuroMatrix project funded by the European Commission (6th Framework Programme.

References

Bertoldi, N., R. Cattoni, et al. (2004). The ITC-irst Statistical Machine Translation System for IWSLT-2004. IWSLT, Kyoto, Japan.

Bilmes, J. A. and K. Kirchhoff (2003). Factored language models and Generalized Parallel Backoff. HLT/NACCL.

Brown, P. F., J. Cocke, et al. (1990). "A statistical approach to machine translation."

Chiang, D. (2005). A hierarchical phrase-based model for statistical machine translation. ACL.

Deng, Y., S. Kumar, et al. (2006). "Segmentation and alignment of parallel text for statistical machine translation." Natural Language Engineering.

Eichelberg, M., J. Riesmeier, et al. (2004). "Ten years of medical imaging standardization and prototypical implementation: the DICOM standard and the OFFIS DICOM toolkit (DCMTK)." Medical Imaging 2004: PACS and Imaging Informatics **5371**: 57-68 (2004).

Fabri, A., G.-J. Giezeman, et al. (2000). "On the Design of CGAL, a Computational Geometry Algorithms Li-

---

[5] moses-support@mit.edu

brary." Software—Practice & Experience **30**(11, Special issue on discrete algorithm engineering).

Koehn, P. (2004). Pharaoh: a Beam Search Decoder for Phrase-Based Statistical Machine Translation Models. AMTA.

Koehn, P., M. Federico, et al. (2006). Open Source Toolkit for Statistical Machine Translation. Report of the 2006 Summer Workshop at Johns Hopkins University.

Koehn, P. and H. Hoang (2007). Factored Translation Models. EMNLP.

Kumar, S. and W. Byrne (2003). A weighted finite state transducer implementation of the alignment template model for statistical machine translation. ACL, Edmonton, Canada.

Liang, P., A. Bouchard-Côté, et al. (2006). An End-to-End Discriminative Approach to Machine Translation. COLING/ACL.

Och, F. J. (2003). Minimum Error Rate Training for Statistical Machine Translation. ACL.

Och, F. J. and H. Ney (2003). "A Systematic Comparison of Various Statistical Alignment Models." Computational Linguistics **29**(1): 19-51.

Och, F. J. and H. Ney (2004). "The alignment template approach to statistical machine translation." Computational Linguistics.

Olteanu, M., C. Davis, et al. (2006). Phramer - An Open Source Statistical Phrase-Based Translator. ACL Workshop on Statistical Machine Translation.

Patry, A., F. Gotti, et al. (2006). Mood at work: Ramses versus Pharaoh. ACL, New York City, USA.

Sadat, F., H. Johnson, et al. (2005). PORTAGE: A Phrase-based Machine Translation System. ACL Workshop on Building and Using Parallel Texts: Data-Driven Machine Translation and Beyond, Ann Arbor, Michigan, USA.

Shen, W., B. Delaney, et al. (2005). The MITLL/AFRL MT System. IWSLT, Pittsburgh, PA, USA.

Shen, Y., C.-k. Lo, et al. (2007). HKUST Statistical Machine Translation Experiments for IWSLT 2007. IWSLT, Trento.

Stolcke, A. (2002). SRILM An Extensible Language Modeling Toolkit. Intl. Conf. on Spoken Language Processing.

Talbot, D. and M. Osborne (2007). Smoothed Bloom filter language models: Tera-Scale LMs on the Cheap. EMNLP, Prague, Czech Republic.

Wang, Z., J. Shawe-Taylor, et al. (2007). Kernel Regression Based Machine Translation. NAACL HLT.

Zens, R. and H. Ney (2007). Efficient phrase-table representation for machine translation with applications to online MT and speech recognition. HLT/NAACL.

Buckwalter-based Lookup Tool as Language Resource for Arabic Language Learners

Jeffrey Micher
Multilingual Computing Branch
Army Research Laboratory
Adelphi, MD 20783 USA
jmicher@arl.army.mil

Clare R. Voss
Multilingual Computing Branch
Army Research Laboratory
Adelphi, MD 20783 USA
voss@arl.army.mil

The morphology of the Arabic language is rich and complex; words are inflected to express variations in tense-aspect, person, number, and gender, while they may also appear with clitics attached to express possession on nouns, objects on verbs and prepositions, and conjunctions. Furthermore, Arabic script allows the omission of short vowel diacritics. For the Arabic language learner trying to understand non-diacritized text, the challenge when reading new vocabulary is first to isolate individual words within text tokens and then to determine the underlying lemma and root forms to look up the word in an Arabic dictionary.

Buckwalter (2005)'s morphological analyzer (BMA) provides an exhaustive enumeration of the possible internal structures for individual Arabic strings in XML, spelling out all possible vocalizations (diacritics added back in), parts of speech on each token identified within the string, lemma ids, and English glosses for each tokenized substring.

The version of our Buckwalter-based Lookup Tool (BBLT) that we describe in this poster provides an interactive interface for language learners to copy and paste, or type in, single or multiple Arabic strings for analysis by BMA (see Fig. 1)

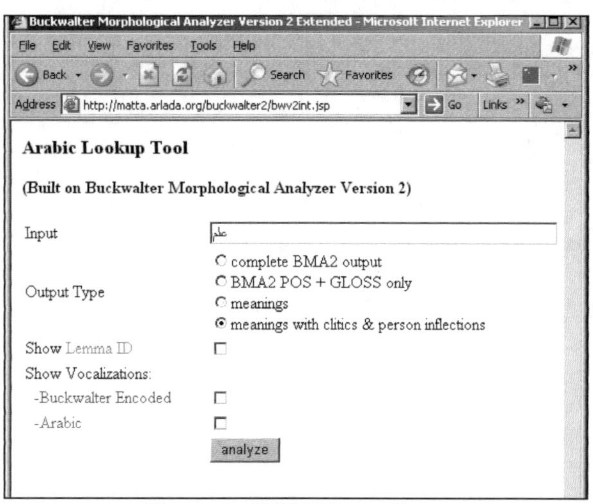

Figure 1. BBLT Input Screen

We originally developed BBLT for ourselves as machine translation (MT) developers and evaluators, to rapidly see the meanings of Arabic strings that were not being translated by our Arabic-English (MT) engines (Voss et al. 2006), while we were also testing synonym lookup capabilities in Arabic WordNet tool (Elkateb et al. 2006). While BBLT allows users to see the "raw" BMA XML (see Fig. 2), the look-up capability that sorts the entries by distinct lemma and presents by English gloss has proved the most useful to English-speaking users who cannot simply lookup Arabic words in the Hans Wehr dictionary (considered the most complete source of Arabic words with about 13,000 entries, but requires the user to be able to "know" the underlying form to search for).

Figure 2. BBLT Output for single token with option "meanings with clitics and person inflections" on

The BBLT user can opt to see the glosses with or without the clitics or inflections, with their diacritized forms either transliterated or rewritten

Software Engineering, Testing, and Quality Assurance for Natural Language Processing, pages 66–67,
Columbus, Ohio, USA, June 2008. ©2008 Association for Computational Linguistics

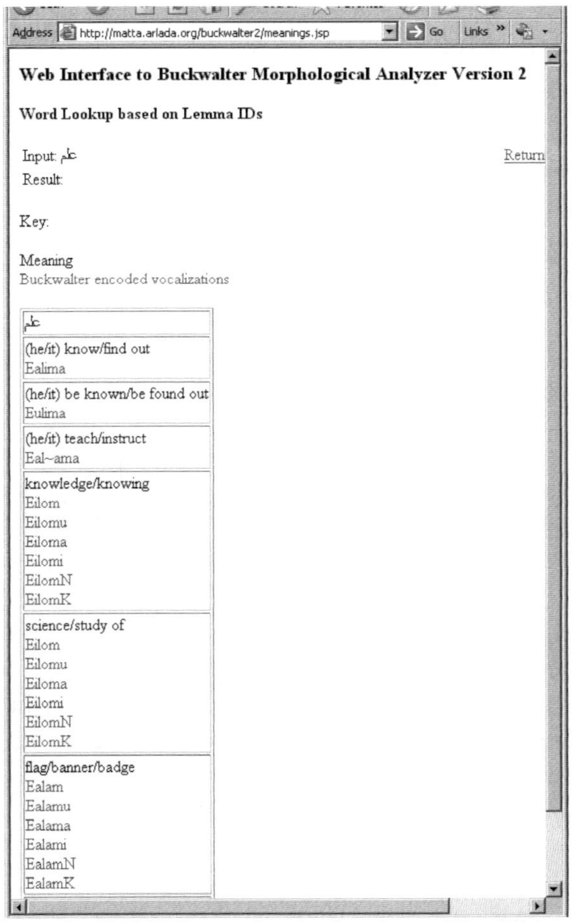

Figure 3. BBLT Output for single token with additional option "Buckwalter encoded vocalizations" on

in Arabic script (see Fig. 3) or in full table form for full sentence glossing (see Fig. 4).

The web application is written as a Java webapp to be run in a tomcat web server. It makes use of wevlets written as both standalone sevlets, extending HttpServlet, and .jsp pages. One servlet handles running BMA as a socket-server process and another servlet handles request from the input .jsp page, retrieves the raw output from the former, process the output according to input page parameters, and redirects the output to the appropriate .jsp page for display.

References

Buckwalter Arabic Morphological Analyzer (BAMA), Version 2.0, LDC Catalog number LDC2004L02, www.ldc.upenn.edu/Catalog.

Buckwalter,T. (2005) www.qamus.org/morphology.htm

Elkateb, S., Black, W., Rodriguez, H, Alkhalifa, M., Vossen, P., Pease, A. and Fellbaum, C., (2006). Building a WordNet for Arabic, in *Proceedings of The fifth international conference on Language Resources and Evaluation (LREC 2006).*

Voss, C., J. Micher, J. Laoudi, C. Tate (2006) "Ongoing Machine Translation Evaluation at ARL," Presentation, In Proceedings of the NIST Machine Translation Workshop, Washington, DC.

Wehr, Hans (1979) Arabic-English Dictionary:: The Hans Wehr Dictionary of Modern Written Arabic. Edited by J. M. Cowan. 4th ed..Wiesbaden, Harrassowitz.

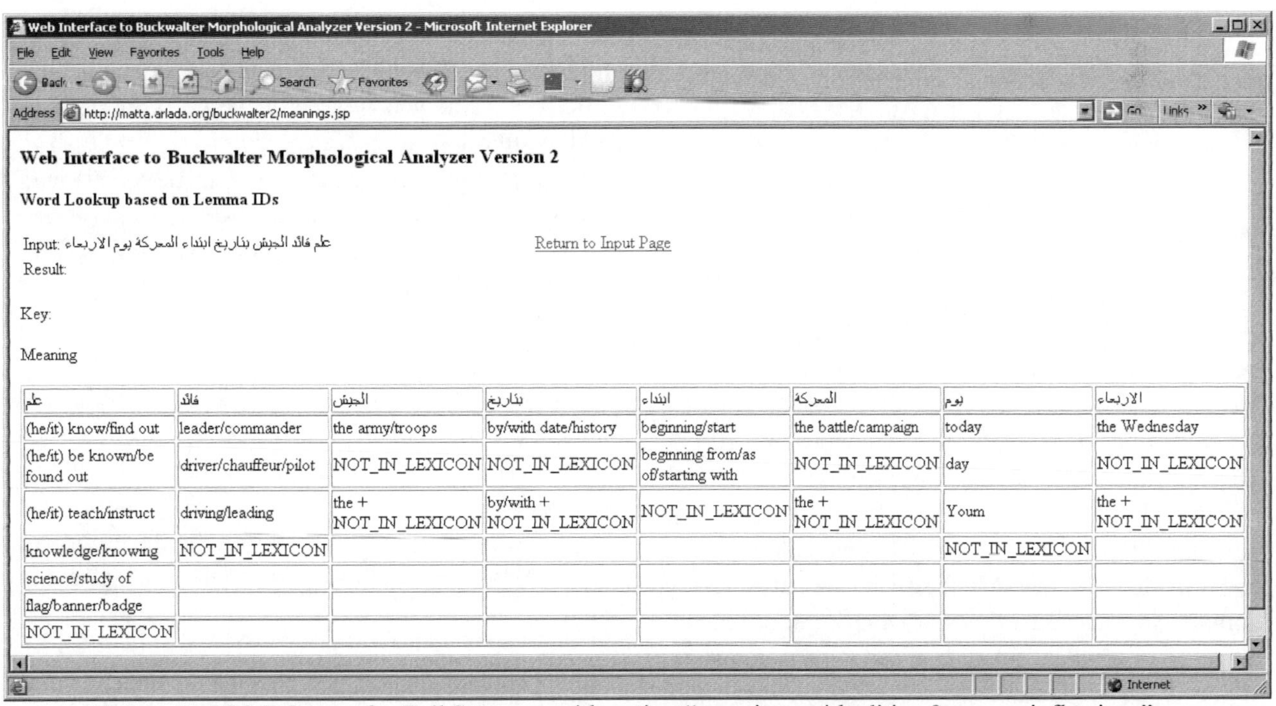

علم	قائد	الجيش	بتاريخ	ابتداء	المعركة	يوم	الاربعاء
(he/it) know/find out	leader/commander	the army/troops	by/with date/history	beginning/start	the battle/campaign	today	the Wednesday
(he/it) be known/be found out	driver/chauffeur/pilot	NOT_IN_LEXICON	NOT_IN_LEXICON	beginning from/as of/starting with	NOT_IN_LEXICON	day	NOT_IN_LEXICON
(he/it) teach/instruct	driving/leading	the + NOT_IN_LEXICON	by/with + NOT_IN_LEXICON	NOT_IN_LEXICON	the + NOT_IN_LEXICON	Youm	the + NOT_IN_LEXICON
knowledge/knowing	NOT_IN_LEXICON					NOT_IN_LEXICON	
science/study of							
flag/banner/badge							
NOT_IN_LEXICON							

Figure 4. BBLT Output for Full Sentence with option "meanings with clitics & person inflections"

Reengineering a domain-independent framework for Spoken Dialogue Systems

Filipe M. Martins, Ana Mendes, Márcio Viveiros, Joana Paulo Pardal, Pedro Arez, Nuno J. Mamede and João Paulo Neto
Spoken Language Systems Laboratory, L^2F – INESC-ID
Department of Computer Science and Engineering,
Instituto Superior Técnico, Technical University of Lisbon
R. Alves Redol, 9 - 2° – 1000-029 Lisboa, Portugal
{fmfm,acbm,mviveiros,joana,pedro,njm,jpn}@l2f.inesc-id.pt
http://www.l2f.inesc-id.pt

Abstract

Our work in this area started as a research project but when L^2F joined TecnoVoz, a Portuguese national consortium including Academia and Industry partners, our focus shifted to real-time professional solutions. The integration of our domain-independent Spoken Dialogue System (SDS) framework into commercial products led to a major reengineering process.

This paper describes the changes that the framework went through and that deeply affected its entire architecture. The communication core was enhanced, the modules interfaces were redefined for an easier integration, the SDS deployment process was optimized and the framework robustness was improved. The work was done according to software engineering guidelines and making use of design patterns.

1 Introduction

Our SDS framework was created back in 2000 (Mourão et al., 2004), as the result of three graduation theses (Cassaca and Maia, 2002; Mourão et al., 2002; Viveiros, 2004), one of which evolved into a masters thesis (Mourão, 2005). The framework is highly inspired on the TRIPS architecture (Allen et al., 2000): it is a frame-based domain-independent framework that can be used to build domain-specific dialogue systems. Every domain is described by a frame, composed by domain slots that are filled with user requests. When a set of domain slots is filled, a service is executed. In order to do so, the dialogue system interacts with the user until enough information is provided.

From the initial version of the framework two systems were created for two different domains: a bus ticket vending system, which provides an interface to access bus timetables; and a digital virtual butler named Ambrósio that controls home devices, such as TVs (volume and channel), acclimatization systems, and lights (switch on/off and intensity) through the X10 electrical protocol and the IrDA (Infrared Data Association) standard. Since 2003, Ambrósio is publicly available in the "House of the Future"[1], on the Portuguese Telecommunications Museum[2].

As proof of concept, we have also built a prototype system that helps the user while performing some task. This was tested for the cooking domain and the automobile reparation domain.

After the successful deployment of the mentioned systems, we began developing two new automatic telephone-based systems: a home banking system and a personal assistant. These are part of a project of the TecnoVoz[3] consortium technology migration to enterprises. To answer to the challenges that the creation of those new systems brought to light, the focus of the framework shifted from academic issues to interactive use, real-time response and real users. Since our goal was to integrate our SDS framework into enterprise products, we started the development of a commercial solution. Nevertheless, despite this

[1] http://www.casadofuturo.org/
[2] http://www.fpc.pt/
[3] http://www.tecnovoz.pt/

Software Engineering, Testing, and Quality Assurance for Natural Language Processing, pages 68–76,
Columbus, Ohio, USA, June 2008. ©2008 Association for Computational Linguistics

new focus, we wanted to maintain the research features of the framework. This situation led to deep changes in the framework development process: as more robust techniques needed to be used to ensure that new systems could easily be created to respond to client requests. From this point of view, the goal of the reengineering process was to create a framework that provides means of rapid prototyping similar to those of Nuance[4], Loquendo[5] or Artificial Solutions[6].

Also, the new systems we wanted to built carried a significant change on the paradigm of the framework: while in the first systems the effects of users' actions were visible (as they could watch the lights turning on and off, for instance) and a virtual agent face provided feedback, in the new scenarios communication is established only through a phone and, being so, voice is the only feedback.

The new paradigm was the trigger to this process and whenever a new issue needed to be solved the best practices in similar successful systems were studied. Not all can be mentioned. The most relevant are described in what follows.

As it was previously mentioned, TRIPS was the main inspiration for this framework. It is a well known and stable architecture that has proven its merits in accommodating a range of different tasks (Allen et al., 2007; Jung et al., 2007). The main modules of the system interact through a Facilitator (Ferguson et al., 1996), similar to the Galaxy HUB[7] (Polifroni and Seneff, 2000) with KQML (Labrou and Finin, 1997) messages. However, in TRIPS, the routing task is decentralized since the sender modules decide where to send its messages. At the same time, any module can subscribe to selected messages through the Facilitator according to the sender, the type of message or its contents. This mechanism makes it easier to integrate new modules that subscribe the relevant messages without the senders' acknowledgment.

Like our framework, the CMU Olympus is a classical pipeline dialog system architecture (Bohus et al., 2007) where the modules are connected via a Galaxy HUB that uses a central hub and a set of rules for relaying messages from one component to the other. It has the three usual main blocks: Language Understanding, through Phoenix parser and Helios confidence-based annotation module, Dialogue Management, through RavenClaw (Raux et al., 2005; Bohus, 2004), and Language Generation, through Rosetta. Recognition is made with Sphinx and synthesis with Theta. The back-end applications are directly connected to the HUB through an included stub.

Some of our recent developments are also inspired in Voice XML[8], in an effort to simplify the framework parameterization and development, required in the enterprise context. Voice XML provides standard means of declarative configuration of new systems reducing the need of coding to the related devices implementation (Nyberg et al., 2002).

Our reengineering work aimed at: i) making the framework more robust and flexible, enhancing the creation of new systems for different domains; ii) simplifying the system's development, debug and deployment processes through common techniques from software engineering areas, such as design patterns (Gamma et al., 1994; Freeman et al., 2004).

By doing this, we are trying to promote the development and deployment of new dialogue systems with our framework.

This paper is organized as follows: Section 2 presents the initial version of the framework; Section 3 describes its problems and limitations, as well as the techniques we adopted to solve them; Section 4 describes a brief empirical evaluation of the reengineering work; finally, Section 5 closes the paper with conclusions and some remarks about future work directions.

2 Framework description

This section briefly presents our architecture, at its initial stage, before the reengineering process. We also introduce some problems of the initial architecture, as they will be later explained in the next section.

[4] `http://www.nuance.com/`

[5] `http://www.loquendo.com/`

[6] `http://www.artificial-solutions.com/`

[7] The Galaxy Hub maintains connections to modules (parser, speech recognizer, back-end, etc.), and routes messages among them. See `http://communicator.sourceforge.net/`

[8] `http://www.w3.org/Voice/`

2.1 Domain Model

The domain model that characterizes our framework is composed by the following entities:

Domain, which includes a frame realization and generalizes the information about several devices;

Frame, which states the subset of slots to fill for a given domain;

Device, which represents a real device with several states and services. Only one active state exists, at each time, for each device;

State, which includes a subset of services that are active when the state is active;

Service, which instantiates a defined frame and specifies a set of slots type of data and restrictions for that service.

When developing a new domain all these entities have to be defined and instantiated.

2.2 Framework architecture

Our initial framework came into existence as the result of the integration of three main modules:

Input/Output Manager, that controls an Automatic Speech Recognition (ASR) module (Meinedo, 2008), a Text-To-Speech (TTS) module (Paulo et al., 2008) and provides a virtual agent face (Viveiros, 2004);

Dialogue Manager, that interprets the user intentions and generates output messages (Mourão et al., 2002; Mourão, 2005);

Service Manager, that provides a dialogue manager interface to execute the requested services, and an external application interface through the device concept (Cassaca and Maia, 2002).

2.3 Input/Output Manager

The Input/Output Manager (IOManager) controls an ASR module and a TTS module. It also integrates a virtual agent face, providing a more realistic interaction with the user. The synchronization between the TTS output and the animated face is done by an audio–face synchronization manager, which generates the visemes[9] for the corresponding TTS phonemes information. The provided virtual agent face is based on a state machine that informs, among others, when the system is "thinking" or when what the user said was not understood.

Besides, a Graphical User Interface (GUI) exists for text interactions between the user and the system. Although this input interface is usually only used for test and debug proposes (as it skips the ASR module), it could be used in combination with speech, if requested by any specific multi-modal system implementation.

The IOManager provides an interface to the Dialogue Manager that only includes text input and output functions. However, the Dialogue Manager needs to rely on other information, such as the instant the user starts to speak or the moment a synthesized sentence ends. These events are useful, for instance, to set and trigger for user input timeouts.

2.4 Dialogue Manager

The architecture of the Dialogue Manager (Figure 1) has seven main modules: a Parser, an Interpretation Manager, a Task Manager, a Behavior Agent, a Generation Manager, a Surface Generation and a Discourse Context.

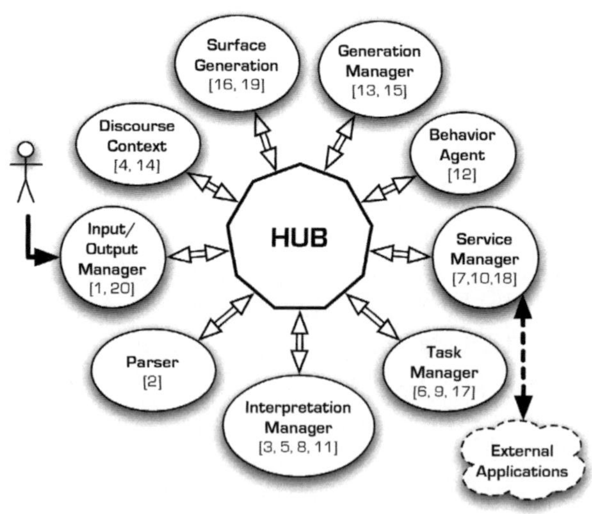

Figure 1: Dialogue Manager architecture through the central HUB. Numbers show the execution sequence.

[9]A *viseme* is the visual representation of a phoneme and is usually associated with muscles positioned near the region of the mouth (Neto et al., 2006).

These modules have specific code from the implementations of the two first systems (the bus ticket vending system and the butler). When building a generic dialogue framework, this situation turns out to be a problem since domain-dependent code was being used that was not appropriate in new systems. Also, the modules have many code for HUB messaging, which makes debug and development harder.

2.5 Service Manager

The Service Manager (Figure 2) was initially developed to handle all domain specific information. It has the following components:

Service Manager Galaxy Server, that works like a HUB stub, managing the interface with the devices and the Dialogue Manager;

Device Manager, that stores information related to all devices. This information is used by the Dialogue Manager to find the service that should be executed after an interaction;

Access Manager, that controls the user access to some devices registered in the system;

Domain Manager, that stores all the information about the domains. This information is used to build interpretations and for the language generation process;

Object Recognition Manager, that recognizes the discourse objects associated with a device;

Device Proxy, abstracts all communication with the Device Core and device specific information protocol. This is done through the *Virtual Proxy* design pattern

Device Core, that implements the other part of the communication protocol with the Service Manager and the Dialogue Manager.

Since the Service Manager interface is shared by the Dialogue Manager and all devices, a device can execute a service that belongs to another device or even access to internal Dialogue Manager information.

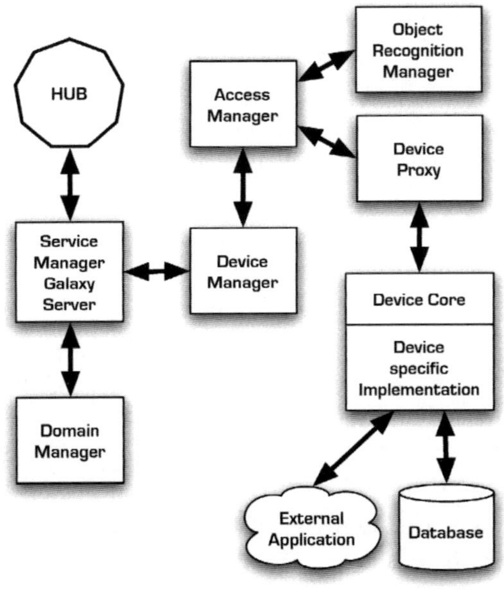

Figure 2: Service Manager architecture.

3 Reengineering a framework

When the challenge of building two new SDSs on our framework appeared, some of the mentioned architectural problems were highlighted. A reengineering process was critical. A starting point for the reengineering process was needed, even though that decision was not clear.

By observing the framework's data and control flow, we noticed that part of the code in the different modules was related with HUB messaging, namely the creation of messages to send, and the conversion of received messages into internal structures (*marshalling*). A considerable amount of time was spent in this task that was repeated across the framework.

Based on that, we decided that the first step should be the analysis of the Galaxy HUB communication flow and the XML structures used to encode those messages, replacing them with more appropriate and efficient protocols.

3.1 Galaxy HUB and XML

The Galaxy HUB protocol is based in generic XML messages. That allows new modules to be easily plugged into the framework, written in any programming language, without modifying any line of code. However, we needed to improve the development and debugging processes of the existing modules, and having a time consuming task that was repeated whenever two modules needed to communicate was a serious drawback.

Considering this, we decided to remove the Galaxy HUB. This decision was enforced by the fact that all the framework modules were written in the Java programming language, which already provides direct invocations and objects serialization through Java Remote Method Invocation (RMI).

The major advantage associated with the use of this protocol, was the possibility of removing all the XML-based messaging that repeatedly forced the creation and interpretation of generic messages in execution time. With the use of RMI, these structures were replaced by Java objects that are interchanged between modules transparently. Not only RMI is native to Java.

This was not a simple task, as the team that was responsible for this process was not the team who originally developed the framework. Because of this, the new team lacked familiarity with the overall code structure. In order to reduce the complexity of the process, it was necessary to create a proper interface for each module removing the several entry points that each one had. To better understand the real flow and to minimize the introduction of new bugs while refactoring the code we made the information flow temporarily synchronous.

The internal structure of each module was redesigned and every block of code with unknown functionality was commented out.

This substitution improved the code quality and both the development and the debugging processes. We believe that it also improved the runtime efficiency of the system, even though no evaluation of the performance was made. Empirically, we can say that in the new version of the system less time is needed to complete a task since no explicit conversion of the objects into generic messages is made.

3.2 Domain dependent code

The code of the Parser, the Interpretation Manager and the Surface Generation modules had domain dependent code and it was necessary to clean it out. Since we were modifying the Galaxy HUB code, we took the opportunity and redesigned that code in the aforementioned modules to make it more generic (and, consequently less domain dependent). Being so, the code cleaning process took place while the Galaxy HUB was being replaced.

We were unable to redesign the domain dependent code. Cases like hard-coded word replacement, used both to provide a richer interpretation of the user utterances and to allow giving a natural response to the user. In such cases, we either isolated the domain specific portions of the code or deleted them, even if the interpretation or generation processes were degraded. It can be recovered in the future by including the domain specific knowledge in the dynamic configuration of the Interpretation and Generation managers as suggested by Paulo Pardal (2007)

An example of this process is the splitting of the parser specific code into several parsers: some domain-dependent, some domain-independent, while creating a mechanism to combine them in a configurable chain (through a pipes and filters architecture). This allows the building of smaller data-type specific parsers that the Interpretation Manager selects to achieve the best parsing result, according to the expectations of the system (Martins et al., 2008). These expectations are created according to the assumption that the user will follow the mixed-initiative dialogue flow that the system "suggests" during its turn in the interaction. The strategy also handles those cases were the user does not keep up with those expectations.

3.3 Dialogue Manager Interface

The enhancements introduced at the IOManager level augmented the amount of the information interchanged between this module and the Dialogue Manager, as it could deal with more data coming from the ASR, TTS and the virtual agent face.

However, the Dialogue Manager Interface was continuously evolving and changing. This lack of stability made it harder to maintain the successive versions completely functional during the process.

Following the software engineering practices, and using the *Template Method* design pattern, we started with the definition of modules interfaces and only after that the implementation code of the methods was written. This allows the simultaneous development of different modules that interact. Only when some conflict is reported, the parallel development processes need to be synchronized resulting in the possible revision of the interfaces. Even when an interface was not fully supported by the Dialogue Manager, it was useful since it lead the IOManager continuous improvements and allowed simultaneous developments in the Dialogue Manager.

In order to ease the creation of this interface, an Input/Output adapter was created. This adapter makes the conversion of the information sent by the IOManager to the Dialogue Manager specific format. Having this, when the information exchanged with the Dialogue Manager changes, the Dialogue Manager Interface does not need any transformation. In addition, the Dialogue Manager is able to interact with other Input/Output platforms without the need of internal changes.

This solution for the interfaces follows the *Facade* design pattern, which provides an unique interface for several internal modules.

3.4 File system reorganization

When the different dialogue systems were fully implemented in the new version of the framework, we wanted to keep providing simultaneous access to the several available domains during the same execution of the system.

In fact, in our initial framework it was already possible to have several different domains running in parallel. When an interaction is domain ambiguous, the system tries to solve the ambiguity by asking the user which domain is being referred.

`User:`	*Ligar*
`System:`	*O que deseja fazer:* *ligar um electrodoméstico* *ou fazer um telefonema?*

Figure 3: Example of a domain ambiguous interaction while running with two different running domains. In Portuguese "*ligar*" means "*switch on*" and "*call*"

Consider the example on Figure 3: an user interaction with two different running domains, the butler and the personal digital assistant. In Portuguese, the verb "*ligar*" means "*to switch something on*" or "*to make a phone call*". Since there are two running domains, and the user utterance is domain ambiguous, the systems requests for a disambiguation in its next turn (*O que deseja fazer*), by asking if the user wants to switch on a home device (*ligar um electrodoméstico*) or make a phone call (*fazer um telefonema*).

While using this feature, it came to our attention that it was necessary to reorganize the file system: the system folder held the code of all domains, and every time we needed to change a specific domain property, we had hundreds of properties files to look at. This situation was even harder for novice framework developers, since it was difficult to find exactly which files needed to be modified in that dense file system structure. Moreover, the ASR, TTS and virtual agent configurations were shared by all domains.

To solve this problem we applied the concept of *system–instance*. A *system–instance* has one or more domains. When the system starts, it receives a parameter that specifies which instance we want to run. The configuration of the existing instances is split across different folders. A library folder was created and organized in external libraries (libraries from an external source), internal libraries (library developed internally at our laboratory) and instance specific libraries (specific libraries of a *system–instance*).

With this organization we improved the versioning management and updates. The conflicting configuration was removed since each *system–instance* has now its own configuration. The configuration files are organized and whenever we need to deliver a new version of a *system–instance*, we simply need to select the files related with it.

3.5 Service Manager redesign

The Service Manager code had too many dependencies with different modules. The Service Manager design was based on the *Virtual Proxy* design pattern. However, it was not possible to develop new devices without creating dependencies on all of the Service Manager code, as the Device Core code relied heavily on some classes of the Service Manager.

This situation created difficulties in the SDSs development process and affected new developments since the Service Manager code needed to be copied whenever a Device Core was running in another computer or in a web container. This is a known bad practice in software engineering, since the code is scattered, making it harder to maintain updated code in all the relevant locations.

It was necessary to split the Service Manager code

for the communication protocol between communication itself and the device specific code.

Also, the Service Manager class[10] interface was shared by the Dialogue Manager and all devices. Being so, it was possible that a device requested the execution of a service in other device, as well as to access the internal information exchanged between the Service Manager and the Dialogue Manager.

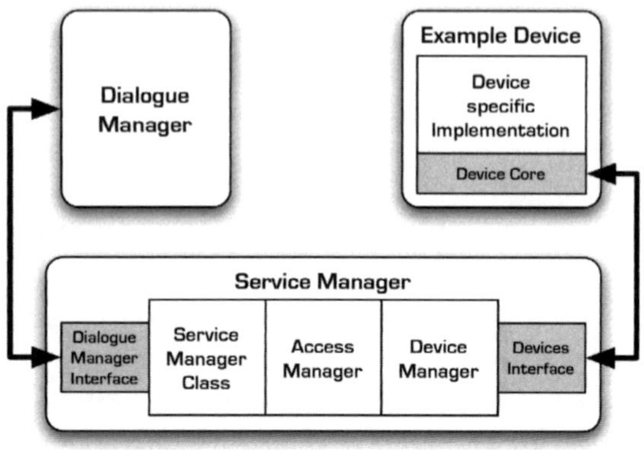

Figure 4: Service Manager architecture.

Like we did with the Dialogue Manager, we specified a coherent interface for the different Service Manager modules, removing the unwanted entry points. The Service Manager class interface was split and the Device Manager is now the interface between the Service Manager and the devices (Figure 4). Also, the Service Manager class interface is only accessed by the Dialogue Manager. The classes between the Service Manager and the Device implementation were organized in a small library, containing the classes and the Device Core code. This library is all what is needed to create a new device and to connect it to both the Service Manager and the Dialogue Manager.

Finally, we changed the Access Manager to control not only user access to registered devices, but also the registry of devices in the system. This prevents a device which is running on a specific *system–instance* to be registered in some other running *system–instance*. This module changed its position in the framework architecture: now it is between the Service Manager class and the Device Manager.

[10]The Service Manager Galaxy Server was renamed to Service Manager. However, we decided to call it here by Service Manager class so it will not be mistaken with the Service Manager module.

3.6 Event Manager

In the initial stage, when the Galaxy HUB was removed, all the communication was made synchronous. After that, to enhance the framework and allow mixed initiative interactions, a mechanism that provides asynchronous communication was needed. Also, it was necessary to propagate information between the ASR, TTS, GUI and the Dialogue System, crucial for the error handling and recovery tasks.

We came to the conclusion that most of the frameworks deal with these problems by using event management dedicated modules. Although TRIPS, the framework that initially inspired ours, has an Event Manager, that was not available in ours. The ASR and TTS modules provided already an event-based information propagation, and we needed to implement a dedicated module to make the access to this sort of information simpler. This decision was enforced by the existence of a requirement on handling events originated by an external Private Branch eXchange (PBX) system, like incoming call and closed call events. The PBX system was integrated with the personal assistant that is available through a phone connection. SDS.

We decided to create an Event Manager in the IOManager. The Dialogue Manager implements an event handler that receives events from the Event Manager and knows where to deliver them. Quickly we understood that the event handler needed to be dependent of the *system–instance* since the events and their handling are different across systems (like a telephone system and kiosk system). With this in mind, we implemented the event handler module, following the *Simple Factory* design pattern, by delegating the events handling to the specific system-instance handler. If this specific *system–instance* event handler is not specified, the system will use a default event handler with "generic" behavior.

This developments were responsible for the continuous developments in the IOManager, referred in section 3.3, and occurred at the same time.

With this approach, we can propagate and handle all the ASR events, the TTS events, GUI events and external applications events.

The Event Manager has evolved to a decentralized HUB. Through this, the sender can set identifiers in some events. These identifiers are used by other modules to identify messages relevant to them. In TRIPS a similar service is provided by the Facilitator, that routes messages according to the recipients specified by the sender, and following the subscriptions that modules can do by informing the Facilitator. This approach eases the integration of new modules without changing the existing ones, just by subscribing the relevant type of messages.

3.7 Dialogue Manager distribution

Currently, there are some clients interested in our framework to create their own SDS. However, since the code is completely written in Java, distributions are made available through `jar` files that can be easily decoded, giving access to the source of our code. To avoid this we need to obfuscate the code.

Even though obfuscation is an interesting solution, our code used Java's *reflexion* in several points. This technique enables dynamic retrieval of classes and data structures by name. By doing so, it needs to know the specific name of the classes being reflected so that the Java class loader knows where to find them. Obfuscation, among other things, changes class names and locations, preventing the Java class loader from finding them.

To cope with this additional challenge, the code that makes use of *reflexion* was replaced using the *Simple Factory* design pattern. This change allows the translation of the hard-coded names to the new obfuscated names in obfuscation time. After that, when some class needs to instantiate one of those classes that used reflection, that instance can be created through the proper factory.

4 Evaluation

Although a SDS was successfully deployed in our initial framework, which is publicly available at a Museum since 2003, no formal evaluation was made at that initial time. Due to this, effective or numeric comparison between the framework as it was before the reengineering work and as it is now, is not possible. Previous performance parameters are not available. However, some empirical evaluation is possible, based on generic principles of Software (re) Engineering.

In the baseline framework, each improvement, like modifications in the dialogue flow or at the parser level, was a process that took more than two weeks of work, of two software engineers. With the new version, similar changes are done in less than one week, by the same team. This includes internal improvements, and external developments made by entities using the system. The system is more stable and reliable now: in the beginning, the system had an incorrect behavior after some hours of running time; currently with a similar load, it runs for more than one month without needing to be restarted.

This is one great step for the adoption of our framework. This stability, reliability and development speed convinced our partners to create their Spoken Dialogue Systems with our framework.

5 Conclusions and Future Work

Currently, our efforts are concentrated on interpretation improvement and on error handling and recovery (Harris et al., 2004).

Currently, we are working on representing emotions within the SDS framework. We want to test the integration, and how people will react to a system with desires and moods.

The next big step will be the inclusion of an efficient morpho-syntactic parser which generates and provides more information (based on speech acts) to the Interpretation Manager.

Another step we have in mind is to investigate how the events and probabilistic information that the ASR module injects in the system can be used to recover recognition errors.

The integration of a Question-Answering (QA) system (Mendes et al., 2007) in this framework is also in our horizon. This might require architectural changes in order to bring together the interpretation and disambiguation features from the SDS with the Information Retrieval (IR) features of QA systems. This would provide information-providing systems through voice interaction (Mendes, 2008).

Another ongoing work is the study of whether ontologies can enrich a SDS. Namely, if they can be used to abstract knowledge sources allowing the system to focus only on dialogue phenomena rather than architecture adaptation, when including new domains (Paulo Pardal, 2007).

Acknowledgments

This work was partially funded by TECNOVOZ, PRIME National Project number 03/165.

It was also partially funded by DIGA, project POSI/PLP/14319/2001 of Fundação para a Ciência e Tecnologia (FCT).

Joana Paulo Pardal is supported by a PhD fellowship from FCT (SFRH/BD/30791/2006).

References

James Allen, Donna Byron, Myroslava Dzikovska, George Ferguson, Lucian Galescu, and Amanda Stent. 2000. An architecture for a generic dialogue shell. *Natural Language Engineering, Cambridge University Press*, 6.

James Allen, Nathanael Chambers, George Ferguson, Lucian Galescu, Hyuckchul Jung, Mary Swift, and William Taysom. 2007. Plow: A collaborative task learning agent. In *Proc. 22th AAAI Conf.* AAAI Press.

Dan Bohus, Antoine Raux, Thomas Harris, Maxine Eskenazi, and Alexander Rudnicky. 2007. Olympus: an open-source framework for conversational spoken language interface research. In *Workshop on Bridging the Gap: Academic and Industrial Research in Dialog Technology*, HLT-NAACL.

Dan Bohus. 2004. Building spoken dialog systems with the RavenClaw/Communicator architecture. Presentation at Sphinx Lunch Talk, CMU, Fall.

Renato Cassaca and Rui Maia. 2002. Assistente electrónica. Instituto Superior Técnico (IST), Universidade Técnica de Lisboa (UTL), Graduation Thesis.

George Ferguson, James Allen, Brad Miller, and Eric Ringger. 1996. The design and implementation of the TRAINS-96 system: A prototype mixed-initiative planning assistant. Technical Report TN96-5.

Elisabeth Freeman, Eric Freeman, Bert Bates, and Kathy Sierra. 2004. *Head First Design Patterns*. O'Reilly.

Erich Gamma, Richard Helm, Ralph Johnson, and John Vlissides. 1994. *Design Patterns: Elements of Reusable Object-Oriented Software*. Addison-Wesley Professional Computing Series.

Thomas Harris, Satanjeev Banerjee, Alexander Rudnicky, June Sison, Kerry Bodine, and Alan Black. 2004. A research platform for multi-agent dialogue dynamics. In *13th IEEE Intl. Workshop on Robot and Human Interactive Communication (ROMAN)*.

Hyuckchul Jung, James Allen, Nathanael Chambers, Lucian Galescu, Mary Swift, and William Taysom. 2007. Utilizing natural language for one-shot task learning. *Journal of Logic and Computation*.

Yannis Labrou and Tim Finin. 1997. A proposal for a new KQML specification. Technical Report CS-97-03, Computer Science and Electrical Engineering Department, Univ. of Maryland Baltimore County.

Filipe M. Martins, Ana Mendes, Joana Paulo Pardal, Nuno J. Mamede, and João Paulo Neto. 2008. Using system expectations to manage user interactions. In *Proc. PROPOR 2008 (to appear)*, LNCS. Springer.

Hugo Meinedo. 2008. *Audio Pre-processing and Speech Recognition for Broadcast News*. Ph.D. thesis, IST, UTL.

Ana Mendes, Luísa Coheur, Nuno J. Mamede, Luís Romão, João Loureiro, Ricardo Daniel Ribeiro, Fernando Batista, and David Martins de Matos. 2007. QA@L2F@QA@CLEF. In *Cross Language Evaluation Forum: Working Notes - CLEF 2007 Workshop*.

Ana Mendes. 2008. Introducing dialogue in a QA system. In *Doctoral Symposium of 13th Intl. Conf. Apps. Nat. Lang. to Information Systems, NLDB (to appear)*.

Márcio Mourão, Pedro Madeira, and Miguel Rodrigues. 2002. Dialog manager. IST, UTL, Graduation Thesis.

Márcio Mourão, Renato Cassaca, and Nuno J. Mamede. 2004. An independent domain dialogue system through a service manager. In *EsTAL*, volume 3230 of *LNCS*. Springer.

Márcio Mourão. 2005. Gestão e representação de domínios em sistemas de diálogo. Master's thesis, IST, UTL.

João Paulo Neto, Renato Cassaca, Márcio Viveiros, and Márcio Mourão. 2006. Design of a Multimodal Input Interface for a Dialogue System. In *Proc. PROPOR 2006*, volume 3960 of *LNCS*. Springer.

Eric Nyberg, Teruko Mitamura, and Nobuo Hataoka. 2002. DialogXML: extending Voice XML for dynamic dialog management. In *Proc. 2th Int. Conf. on Human Language Technology Research*. Morgan Kaufmann Publishers Inc.

Sérgio Paulo, Luís C. Oliveira, Carlos Mendes, Luís Figueira, Renato Cassaca, Céu Viana, and Helena Moniz. 2008. DIXI - A Generic Text-to-Speech System for European Portuguese. In *Proc. PROPOR 2008 (to appear)*, LNCS. Springer.

Joana Paulo Pardal. 2007. Dynamic use of ontologies in dialogue systems. In *NAACL-HLT Doctoral Consortium*.

Joseph Polifroni and Stephanie Seneff. 2000. GALAXY-II as an architecture for spoken dialogue evaluation. In *Proc. 2nd Int. Conf. Language Resources and Evaluation (LREC)*.

Antoine Raux, Brian Langner, Dan Bohus, Alan Black, and Maxine Eskenazi. 2005. Let's go public! taking a spoken dialog system to the real world. In *Proc. INTERSPEECH*.

Márcio Viveiros. 2004. Cara falante – uma interface visual para um sistema de diálogo falado. IST, UTL, Graduation Thesis.

Author Index

Association for Computational Linguistics
209 N. Eighth Street
Stroudsburg, Pennsylvania 18360

CURRAN ASSOCIATES INC
proceedings.com